Jean Nutter

FIRST LOVE

22 April 1979.

Affectionately inscribed
to Duncan on his 21st
birthday by the author.

Leslie Paul

FIRST LOVE
A journey

LONDON
SPCK

First published 1977
SPCK
Holy Trinity Church
Marylebone Road
London NW1 4DU

Printed in Great Britain by
Billing & Sons Limited, Guildford, London and Worcester

ISBN 0 281 02975 X

For
Norman Goodacre
in homage

What a long way I had gone, round and round the houses,
only to come back to the most intense conviction,
to the first and greatest love of my life.
                                        ANGRY YOUNG MAN

CONTENTS

ACKNOWLEDGEMENTS

The sources of the quotations which head the six parts of my book are as follows: the first I wrote myself for the Woodcraft Folk when I was a boy; the second comes from Siegfried Sassoon's 'Everyone Sang' in *Collected Poems 1908-1956* (Faber 1961); Thomas Traherne is the author of the third, which comes from 'The Salutation' in his *Poetical Works* (Dobell 1932); as to the fourth, this is the Russian proverb passionately advanced by Alexander Solzhenitsyn in his Nobel Prize Lecture (Stenvalley Press 1973); Dylan Thomas is of course the author of the Part Five heading (*Collected Poems 1934-1952*, Dent 1952); and the heading to Part Six I borrowed from George Steiner's *In Bluebeard's Castle* (Faber 1971).

My thanks are due to the following for permission to quote from copyright sources:

Geoffrey Bles Ltd: *The Divine and the Human* by Nicolas Berdyaev.

Cambridge University Press: *Three Traditions of Moral Thought* by Dorothea Krook.

Faber & Faber Ltd: 'Spain, 1937' in *Collected Shorter Poems 1930-1944* (Copyright by W.H. Auden 1945), and 'In Memory of W.B. Yeats' in *Collected Shorter Poems 1927-1957* (Copyright 1940 and renewed 1968 by W.H. Auden), both by W.H. Auden (US rights by permission of Random House Inc.); 'The Waste Land', 'The Love Song of J. Alfred Prufrock', 'The Hollow Men', 'Ash Wednesday', 'Preludes', 'Morning at the Window' in *Collected Poems 1909-1962* by T.S. Eliot (US rights by permission of Harcourt Brace Jovanovich Inc.); *In Bluebeard's Castle: Or Some Notes Towards a Re-definition of Culture* by George Steiner (US rights by permission of Yale University Press).

Hughes Massie Ltd for the Roy Campbell Estate: 'Verses written after an ecstasy of high exaltation' in *Poems of St. John of the Cross*, translated by Roy Campbell.

The Loeb Classical Library (Harvard University Press: William Heinemann): Plato's *Gorgias*, translated by W.R.M. Lamb.

The Estate of Harold Owen, Chatto & Windus Ltd, and New Directions Publishing Corporation: 'Anthem for Doomed Youth' and 'Dulce et Decorum Est' in *Collected Poems* by Wilfred Owen, copyright Chatto & Windus Ltd, 1946, ©1963.

Pitman Publishing Ltd: *Karl Marx: Selected Writings in Sociology and Social Philosophy*, ed. T.B. Bottomore and M. Rubel. (Published by C.A. Watts 1956.)

George Sassoon Esq. and Viking Press Inc.: 'Everyone Sang' in *Collected Poems 1908-1956* by Siegfried Sassoon, Copyright 1920 by E.P. Dutton & Co., 1948 by Siegfried Sassoon.

M.B. Yeats, Miss Anne Yeats, The Macmillan Company of London and Basingstoke, The Macmillan Publishing Company Inc., New York: 'The Second Coming' in *The Collected Poems of W.B. Yeats* (Copyright 1924 by the Macmillan Company, renewed 1952 by Bertha Georgie Yeats).

Biblical quotations are in general taken from the New English Bible, second edition ©1970, by permission of Oxford and Cambridge University Presses.

Thanks are also due to the following for consenting to the reproduction of material from my previous published works:

The Caravel Press: 'Poem' and 'Invocation' from *Exile and Other Poems*.

The C.W. Daniel Co. Ltd: 'The Song of Creation' from *The Pipes of Pan*.

Hodder & Stoughton and A.P. Watt & Son: *Traveller on Sacred Ground*.

Outposts Publications: *Journey to Connemara and Other Poems*.

I wish to thank Ruby Gordon for wrestling with many re-typings and Miss Jean Nutter for reading for errors. I am deeply grateful to Norman Goodacre and Eric James for constant encouragement.

PART ONE

Now doth the blackness of night encircle us
WOODCRAFT FOLK FIRE CEREMONY

It was in the night, and in the middle way of life, that I found myself uncontrollably weeping. My diabetes and the virus illness which followed it had brought me to the point where I could see no way out or round. I had no strength left. In lucid exhaustion I lay alone and spread-eagled on my bed. I could promise myself, I thought sadly, thinking of years fled, the chance of living another year, and so of completing the research task laid upon me: not more. I wanted to finish it, but no longer (just then) cared for life beyond that point. Why then was I weeping? For sheer helplessness, of course, before a condition that made me weaker day by day, without quite knocking me off my feet and putting me in hospital, or which stayed its hand for a few days, and sent up my spirits, then returned more vile than before. Yet not only for this reason. I was basely afraid of not being able to live as a man, on my own two feet, but I was not so afraid to die. Since the war I had come to see, with relief, that the more one loved life, the more necessary the closure of death was. One could have love, too, beyond the bearing.

I could not stay my tears by argument. I am having a break-down, I thought, wondering how serious it was, and I was ashamed. What could I do if discovered like this? I had wept so seldom and only twice before like this. I had none of the usual symptoms of depression, such as a sense of futility or hopelessness, but rather of being defeated in my struggle to go on in self-will. The counterforce was too strong and had thrown me, pinning me by the shoulders. I remembered Charles Péguy — that superb poet, supporter of Dreyfus, killed at the Battle of the Marne — weeping on the tops of Parisian omnibuses as he told his beads, for love of the Church from which he was excommunicated. I remember Emmanuel Mounier, with the grave thoughtful working-man's face, and the artisan's hands and a grip like iron, for all too short a while my friend, who died weeping, or so they said. No, he did not *die weeping*, he died *from* weeping, consumed by this grief for himself and for the world on which he had flung himself with so much ardour and love and towards which he held out hands which now said, 'I have done all I can. I can do no more. It is not enough, God forgive me!' and died with his tears baptizing him. And surely Simone Weil, keeping her appointment with God in the Grosvenor Sanatorium, wept too, heavy with her death wish, her self-accusing, her God-forsakenness.

I remembered myself as a boy of sixteen or seventeen on that lonely hilltop of a still rural Forest Hill looking down on the street glitter and sombre glow of a London, set free from war, which the low scudding clouds reflected. It was a place, beyond the street lamps, I often came to. That night it was the people boxed in those endless rooms, in those endless uniform streets, not the fascination of the impersonal city, which caught me, and I was flooded through with warmth for them, and found myself weeping. *For* them? Who knows? I could not explain my grief to myself. I was too young and callow to take the measure of my desolation. It was not so much remembered sorrows that moved me (in wartime there had been many of these), but boyhood gone, and fear of all that one had to become to tread resolutely, let alone to master, in that iron land. But the grief that racked me and shocked me was for them and not for myself as I lived it.

As a young boy I had picked up for a halfpenny at a Church bazaar an illustrated history of England with its covers and title page gone so that I never knew the name of the author. Fine steel engravings showed armoured kings and nobles leading hosts into battles. Strong castles, ships of the line, coronation processions, the martyrdom of saints, executions at Tower Hill, these were the meat of the illustrator, and attracted me, for I was at an age when I thought a book without pictures no book at all. The work, or such as I read of it, filled me with melancholy, even grief. A king would arise, handsome, high-spirited, full of courage, to lead his people to battle for glory or against the invader, as Arthur did. His hosts would glitter around him, their lances shaking, his people throng to him. What could gainsay him after 'the enemy broke and fled'? *Everything* could gainsay him! The enemy could recover, his allies defect, his people grow sullen or disaffected, rivals appear. He could fall ill with fever and die on a pilgrimage, be taken in conspiracy and flung into the

4

Tower, receive an assassin's knife between his ribs, or die in himself so that the prince I was ready to love became himself the king-monster I had to loathe. Even when a king was blessed with a long reign of peace and contentment and died, bearded and in bed, his stricken kin kneeling around him, the most intense anxiety rose within me. What then, when he died? Who would protect the realm? Would his heirs be at each other's throats, his inheritance be squandered, faction and civil war arise? Out of everything, no matter how good and glorious at the start, came the ruinous events.

I began each chapter with a beating heart. No matter who you are now, how high your glory, I told the present hero, I have only to turn a few pages to find you clawed down in disaster or dishonour or death. It was the theme I was later to find in Greek tragedy. It is no good: the fates will turn against you as they turned against Oedipus. How strange that it was in this nameless potted history rather than in the scriptures that, so young, so early, I discovered in a search for heroes the desperateness of the human condition. The Gospels reinforced it. No matter what the rejoicing of angels, shepherds and wise men with their lavish gifts, there would come the slaughter of babies in Bethlehem. The Christ-child hurrying to Egypt and safety would return to the doom of the dreaded crucifixion which God did nothing to avert, which made every Good Friday a deep misery for me.

The Great War rubbed that disillusion into the grain of my soul. I had seen on the faces of wounded men, in the hospitals I worked in as a very small boy, that simple men paid the same toll in death and mutilation as princes, without even the preparatory glory.

There were the soldiers in Lewisham Hospital. 'Ah'll nivver go dahn t'pit agen!' Private Eagle used to complain as he propelled his invalid chair about the ward. He was from Paradise Row and a private in the South Staffs, a regiment I was myself eventually to join. He had lost a leg and on his first days in the ward would scream unmercifully as the stump, as raw as beef, was dressed. It unhinged the mind and I would run outside.

There were German soldiers in our hospital, among them a small group of officers who, with the dignity of panthers, delicate and dangerous, paced unwearyingly the small yard between two wings in which they exercised. Their strange uniforms glittered. There was one not as the rest, a U-boat Commander, scruffy, unshaved, with an old woollen scarf round his neck, who trotted round with short steps, his head bent over his Bible.

He was not in his right mind. One day someone ran into the ward. 'The U-boat Commander's just jumped off the balcony.' Quick as a flash I slipped out and ran towards the place of the suicide though what I hoped to see or do, I did not know. As I turned the corner towards the balcony, from which shouts were still coming, an armed guard was standing there looking down at the body, a heap of crumpled clothes at the foot of the fire-escape with guards standing round it arguing, their faces hot with exertion and annoyance. In the midst of the group I saw the pale sad face of the U-boat Commander turned upwards, his piercing blue eyes still open and staring at the foreign sky with surprise and grief.

A guard ran towards me with a rifle. 'Get out of 'ere, scouty,' he said, with menaces. 'Get out before I give you a clout that'll knock you into Saturday week.'

There was a gentle boy in the Australian Army, Arthur Bourke, who came to stay with us. I made friends with him and took him for walks and he left us and went to the front. I wrote him a very proud, full letter. It came back unopened with an official stamp on it, 'Killed in Action.' He had been blown to pieces on his first day at the front and not a trace of him found. I had ended my letter with a scroll bearing the motto 'Nil desperandum'. How did I learn so early that it was so easy, even so obligatory, to despair?

And so it is proper to ask what it was, deeper than melancholy, which plunged the tireless and merry boy of *The Boy Down Kitchener Street* into unexpected heartbreak on that wooded hill. One would ask it with such concern of a son or a godson, of any life almost wholly innocent. And now the same trembling grief had overcome me again. Of course, it was more than forty years later. One no longer had the excuse of innocence and had the right to be worn out by the struggle to accomplish what it was in one to accomplish. That brought tears, as once foreknowledge of what was going to be demanded of one had done. But just as then it was everyman's grief, so it was now. I could look back on my own life and say — so much hope and eagerness and discipline and denial and sheer work, all down the years, always renewed, caught up and pursued perseveringly down the decades, and justified and boasted about and held up as the meaning and purpose of my life! At the end, so little to show that life itself never seemed to have been lived at all, but only something else, a pseudo-life, while the real thing glided silently away beyond the line of willows where one did not trespass; such pitiful triumphs even where one had struggled most! And yet though all this was steel true, and a man must be a blockhead who has never once wept for a life despoiled, it was not only for my own ego in disarray that I wept. I had the same anguished sense now as when a boy, of all that is asked of men down the years, down the centuries, the hopes and desires and ambitions and all the years smashed, flattened, steamrollered by time, and the losses, the wasted energies, the crumbled greatness, remembered at the end like once-fine vessels of royal tables identified only by useless shards; of the individual meanness and corruption, the spite and viciousness of men towards each other, and of the endless tide of violence and terror and cruelty rolled on the world and rolling it on decade by decade, as though this was the only climate in which man truly found himself and other aspiration was fraud or delusion. It was for this human condition that I wept in the absolute silence and stillness of my dark room in the middle of that icily lit London I had once looked down on, trembling.

Griefs such as these, going so deep and seeming without cause, mark life absolutely in its chapters. I knew this was such a new chapter, even if it was no more than what they called having a breakdown (as though one were a motor car with a puncture). Yet as my grief did not lessen through the night, but rather mounted, while my white clarity increased, I saw that there was an element in it, perhaps the strongest, welling up into my consciousness, compellingly, which at first I had not understood. It was felt also when, a boy, I leaned forward on my hill into the west wind blowing through the trees, blowing over London. It had to do with God. It was the presence of God. Or, not to be presumptuous, and to accept one's shyness and recoil as elements easily misunderstood, it was the *question* of the presence of God. Of joy in God? Yes, joy too. So strange. Was it something I was even for a moment prepared to admit to myself? I was well versed in the phrases of conventional piety, the religious jargon, worn so smooth that they cushion us from the actual truth we are supposed to be talking about. I knew too how to retreat behind the barriers of subjectivity and to bring myself to think that everything was happening inside me. Not for nothing was I a child of empiricism. And I suppose that, too, would be more comforting if we knew what the mysterious inwardness we all possess means. But *the* presence? It was a bleak moment in that night which began so badly and surfaced to a limpid acceptance.

It had nothing to do with my illness. No, that is wrong. The halt to the daily business of life which illness brings had provided the clairvoyance as well as the occasion. Then, resting the day before, I had listened to some Gelineau psalms sung at Downside Abbey, and at the melancholy and plaintive Psalm 41, 'My Soul is thirsting for the Lord when shall I see him face to face?', I was caught with vertigo, as when one is overpowered with work and a secretary reminds one of urgent but forgotten, harassing business. In this unexpected grief itself, and through it, I could see my life in a perspective equally unexpected. I felt overwhelmed by the extent to which I had seemed to mistake everything. 'I have completely misunderstood my own life,' I said out loud with more conviction in my heart than in my voice. I had lived it, I saw, to love here and achieve there, to be accepted, to make my mark, to get recognition, to get by — all the things one says, and means at the time, and in an ordinary human sense genuinely needs, things not to be despised. I knew myself to be as worldly as the next man in this context, and was ordinarily prepared to defend myself. I had no defence just then. I was judged.

So often, anyway, defence is shadow boxing: flailing my own shadow and feeling virtuous about it, I could forget the real opponent and postpone for a time the hour when I should have to wrestle, like Jacob, with my angel in the darkness. I now felt, with an anguish which turned my bowels, at this moment of presented insight, that I had lost the true perspective on my life. I now felt, or was forced to feel, because my life seemed that night destroyed, and only honesty was left, that what I had lived by, or wanted to, almost without knowing it, since my childhood, a private and inadmissible hunger, was the sense of the presence of God. I knew too that I had evaded it and its full impact for me since who knows when, by all the means in my power, even religious means, because it was too much to bear. Such was the clairvoyance of that unsummoned invalid grief, and the source of it. What hurt was the conviction of the denial of God and the treachery to my own self of that denial. Perhaps too that the truth was better than any prayer; that my grief was prayer enough.

The discovery, like the discovery of loving someone one thought it impossible to love, did not stop my weeping or even make it easier to bear. It was a new source of despair that one could be so wrong about one's whole life. Yet now through it all was a small point of light, dazzling like the pencil of light which the oculist in his consulting room throws at the pupil of the eye and which at first it instinctively dodges, then learns to accept. It was amazing that I should be so penetrated at this moment in such a way, the light playing on and exposing the nerve of grief. It was with stupefaction that I fell asleep. If I am dying, I thought, this is a strange way to go about it. In recollection it appears a moment of healing, for presently I grew better and would have forgotten that I was even ill, as I usually do, had it not been for the question which was posed to me in the dark wood and was still there, unanswered, when I came out into the light of the common day: and the remembered, the frightening tears.

What stood out in the new perspective backwards to childhood, the black hours uncovered, were those moments when I was taken unawares by experiences different in quality from workaday ones. They were numinous moments: something was on fire in them. They possessed for me Traherne's poetry of the gates of the world. The apprehension of the divine trembled in them. Looking back, they stood out like white peaks above a plain.

It is so easy to deceive one's self. I am afraid even now to give substance to something which ought not to be hypostatized. I never spoke of the tears of my boyhood, for I did not understand them and they were vaguely discreditable. It did not fit the persona of the young rebel I had fashioned for myself to live by. Glory, yes: weeping, no. Nor, and for perhaps the same reason, have I spoken till now of the second breakdown. And even so, now that both are told, what do they prove? That a chivalrous boy was overcome by compassion for other men? That a man in his prime grew sad at the contemplation of the vanished years and wept for himself? If that were all, there would be nothing more to say. I know that what was pressed upon me was much more — a conviction not lightly to be thrown down, that whatever my nominal state of belief or unbelief, I had lived all my life with a sense of the presence of God and of evading the presence of God, of which certain events were the peaks. It was a question of evidence, of how one looked at it, like the essay John Wisdom wrote about 'Gods'[1] in which he used a parable of great beauty concerning a garden. Two people return to their neglected gardens, and find a few old plants thriving vigorously among the weeds. One exclaims that a gardener must have been at work, but the other denies it — but the dispute is not about the evidence, but about the significance of it if it is arranged in this pattern or that. In my case the evidence was all known and for a long time. What the grief-wrought revelation had done was to arrange it in an unexpected pattern of significance. I trembled for its safety. Was it the brittle lucidity of illness, or genuinely a new understanding? It was like looking at the beauty of a kaleidoscope. One twist and the satisfying design would go, never to be renewed. I feared to meddle with experiences which might never yield their being to words, and fear still that I can make appear drab and pitiable a cloth which had to my sight the texture of gold. I fear too the God-words we so easily rattle around, like the battered plastic counters of a game children play because

---

[1] In *Logic and Language*, ed. A.G.N. Flew. Blackwell 1951.

they are too idle to learn another. I feared to speak of hitherto secret things, then find in them another personality asset,
a God-status symbol. It is easier to be humble if one has no
itch to write. It is also easier to be barren. Perhaps one ought
to paint what one sees, or set it to music, or twist it in pieces
of wire and so avoid the snare of words. Certainly 'one had
to know what one sees, above all one had to *see* what one
sees'.

3

I was a religious boy, but not a good one. Goodness, to our
wild boyish world, was a condition of deficiency, like deafness or a limp, its possessor pitied for his affliction. I lied, I
stole when in need, I evaded authorities, I savaged around
with a temper like a blunted sword. My sex was a dangerous
thing to myself and to others. Yet, ignoring the 'goodness' we
equated with spinelessness, we held to specific virtues with a
passionate tenacity: loyalty, courage, spirit, clean language,
honour. There was something in our world then, poor though
it was, which has quite gone since. We had rather go home
blooded, or die even, than have *honour* put to the question,
no better or worse in this than a hundred thousand other
boys of our scouting generation. But what did it mean to be
a religious boy? Nothing, I fancy, that brought much consolation to any person I knew then. It was a dimension one lived
rather than a thing one did on Sundays, say, or kneeling at
one's bedside. I said my prayers regularly, with the candle
flickering behind me, watching the heaving shadows through
my fingers lest I lost control of them and they swirled to
disaster. I held God to account in my prayers, half anxious
and half minatory, pleading with a friend of uncertain mood,
in the spirit of the small boy who dropped his slice of bread
and jam at a party, and shut his eyes in wild prayer, and
opened them to see his slice spread jam side down on the best
carpet. 'God would', he said quietly. 'God would.'
     As a little boy I liked going to evensong with my mother.
The atmosphere, the peripheral things excited me most, the
hissing and popping gas globes, the half-dark vault, the

11

swaying of cross and banner in procession at festival times above the heads of the dense congregation, and the organ in tumult. I longed for martial hymns and a clamorous music. Countless toccatas and fugues thundered down on me: I should have been offended to learn that someone had actually composed them. They demanded to be understood as spirited improvizations on the mood of God that day, drawn down from the stars rather than as sheets of music the organist read. In any case my religion was Manichean. My Lord had to be the great God of the *Venite* and a great king above all gods: it was splendid to think of him standing above Israel, the four corners of the earth in his hands, slaying the thousands and ten thousands of the enemies of Israel, and to sing 'Onward Christian soldiers Marching as to war,' and wonder why one needed the qualifying 'as'.

The cosmic drama was important to me for my sanity, because of my Auntie Florrie. She was a spiritualist possessed of so uncanny a prescience about ghosts and souls of the dead that she went off and founded a spiritualist church in Los Angeles. She handled psychic phenomena in the planchette and table rapping and other routines she taught me with the complacency of a matron dispensing buttered muffins and Mothers' Union tea, and with no idea of the terror they inspired. I was a haunted little boy, who hastily denied it, and the Lord God of Israel, enthroned above the earth so high that men were but ants beneath him, was a rallying point for my depressed spirits. With such a God about, it was less likely that Auntie Florrie's grave-born spirits would be allowed to continue to burrow through our substantial world like termites till it crumbled. Unlike Auntie's, Church religion then was a drama lived publicly, out in the open, repeating itself year after year, full of didacticism and the menace of hell for defaulters, and enjoyed by the congregation of the exclusive who fed on the body and blood of Jesus. With the most tremendous liturgy, in superb language, this public thing rolled over us. Even my prayers were public, said often enough aloud at the bedside with my brother, on the other side of the room, listening mockingly for his *bête-noire*, the split infinitive. Language and drama fed my imagination, and gave me ammunition to deal with Auntie Florrie, bland, dreamy, merciless in her persistence. Yet what went on within me, in the silences of inner space which are more frightening than those galactic spaces which scared Pascal, belonged to another world, then quite inexpressible, and seeming to owe nothing to the institutional religion in which by my mother's care I had been so well brought up. The postulation of so sharp a dichotomy is perhaps insensitive: my imagination fed as avidly upon the Christian felicities as upon poetry presented to me in other ways, with who knows what chemistry of the mind fizzing away in the unconscious and making me a child obsessed with a sense of holiness abroad in the world.

A boy lives much of his life in a noonday world where everything is clear and ordinary and controllable and can be named. In one part of him at least he prefers this uncomplicated world. There's no fooling it: it is full of verifiable entities like houses and trams, and games with rules, like football, the morning bathroom order, the school curriculum. But it is also the source of his major anxieties. What anxious little boys we were, Charles Péguy once said of his own schooldays in Chartres. We wrestled endlessly with the baffling trivia of life — how to get to school on time, how to think of *anything* to say in an essay, how to avoid hated enemies and loathed masters, and to contrive even one word with the friend whose mere presence in the same room changed the quality of its light, how to. . . it was always 'how to' in face of the rules, the programmes, the watching, didactic, vindictive adults. The noonday world was the daylight prison, in which, shabby and furtive, bootlaces undone, ears dirty, stockings in holes, under hammering pressures we shrank and became less than ourselves. There was no time for me even to stop and catch my breath. Only alone, living something not forbidden (if forbidden, adults were present vicariously and that destroyed the precious solitude), was it possible to recollect myself.

What joy when the moment of solitary self-discovery occurred. It came almost with vertigo. I felt my soul enlarge. My body grew about me and took deep satisfactory breaths. I seemed physically to ascend, to leave the ground. A triumphant cock crowed in my head. At last I could discover what 'I' was about. It was not so imperative to shut out the noonday world as to see it with unclouded eyes.

There was a moment of insight one damp spring morning in an enchanting wood close to home, early morning mist smoking round the boles of trees. Our suburb was not wholly built up. Green fingers of the country still probed it. The wide, wild banks of the railways were refuges for hawks and owls and even foxes. We played cricket and rougher games on fields from which the war had banished the builder. The wood was just another survivor. (It has gone now.) I cannot think how it was that I was there so early in the morning unless it was another episode in the solitary mooning around, full of an inward excitement, to which I was as prone as Richard Jefferies. A gentleman came through the wood, for there was a path, going for the train I suppose, and he gave a half smile and nod to me. The ferrule of his umbrella stuck at each prod in the soft mud of the path and came out again with a solemn plop. I watched his departing, respectable back and listened to his musical umbrella. As he went he drew stillness down over the wood again, and the utter solitariness made me tingle and tremble.

I became conscious then of the wood's existence as something quite apart from me or the city gentleman. If I were still enough, I felt, I would hear the whole wood groaning and straining to the sun above the low morning cloud, rotating itself like the sunflower to catch the burning sun in its net of springing leaves. The bird song was the self-communion of the wood, as a boy might whistle himself along to school just for company. As I listened — so intently that I can still hear the blackbird, the greenfinch, the thrush, the chaffinch, the wood pigeon — I entered a new world of experience. Beyond my deafening wood chorus there were other answering bird voices, remote but strong, and farther away still more, faint but penetrating, and far, far, far away, bird song, as remote as clouds, which thin and clear as the horns of Elfland trembled on the verge of hearing itself. And beyond that still more, more, I became certain: a canopy of sound above my head, above my suburb, above the secret country I flew over, an endless chanting roof to human existence.

I was spellbound in the face of this mysterious infinity, so confident, so aloof, so indifferent to me. Something of the egotism of the small boy was broken then, even though one put the experience aside to be considered later, like other

14

half-comprehended things. I saw, at moments, that the world did not revolve round me. Here were other worlds I longed to penetrate and they were alight with glory. In this upward surge of life which had exploded my spirit I saw the wood as one living thing and it filled me with awe. I was full of the privileged delight of a small boy let into a grown-up's secret.

The spell was broken by the steam trains shuddering up from New Cross and London Bridge and by the street clatter of the milkman. Yet the experience remained. Perhaps this childish fever for nature was inevitable in one whose mentors were even then Wordsworth and Tennyson. I am not sure. My friends did not seem to possess it. If now, with age, it has faded and it is the life and strife of man which possess me like a passion, it has been so much the stuff of my days that in this confession I must write as much about nature as about God or my grieving self.

It is true that I used to fly. The moment head touched pillow I was away and into an unknown countryside, effortlessly exploring it, riding the level at hawk height, beating over hedges, the scent of fool's parsley in my nostrils, the wind running its fingers through me, soaring down from green rounded hills to dark tree-lined ravines or rising till the lanes and hamlets were plotted, as on the maps of the earth that air travel was to reveal to me so much later. So convinced was I of the reality of this country I nightly explored that I took a friend on foot to walk down the lane which I knew joined it to my noonday world. To my chagrin I never found it. But even now, all these years later, writing about it has aroused once again the infantile conviction that it was there, just about where I thought it was, if only I had been more persistent in seeking it out. Unless Aunt Florrie's psychical forces had been playing me tricks and I had been exploring a genuine countryside, but of a time before our suburb was built upon it! How else explain its geographical consistency night after night? But what was dream and what was reality? I dreamed of things before they happened, and then they happened as I dreamed them. I dreamed of things and was so convinced they had happened that I dared never assume otherwise, and do not know to this day for certain what was dream and what was event. There were events of such a dreamlike quality that as I looked upon them I thought they would switch off at any moment, and the reliable noonday world move in and take possession, crumbling the ineffable with heavy fingers.

My friend, Jack Pruddah, who was fair and grey-eyed and had dazzling teeth, came to me in a dream. He was ten and I was ten. In the dream we met outside the Chandos, the local pub, and he said straightaway in his anxious way, 'I've got to go away, Les. I've got to go to Ongar school. They're sending me as a boarder, so Les. . . ' And he stopped. My little heart stopped too. I must have looked as pale and anxious as he. I could think of nothing to say. 'Will it be like the *Gem* and the *Magnet* . . . ?' I began and then the dream faded. The next day the dream was still with me, so strongly that I became convinced it was not a dream but a happening and I avoided my friend for I was too full of sorrow to speak to him. Then, on the Saturday, I met him again near the Chandos and he caught my arm and said, 'Les, I've got to go away. I've got to go to Ongar school, Les. They're sending me as a boarder, Les.' And I looked humbly at the pavement and said, my heart stopping, 'I know'. We stared at each other. What could be done with a reality so baffling?

What happened in church and in school, or even when I read the romantic poets, was at someone else's instance or contrivance. I saw quite dutifully what I was supposed to learn and believe. In the experience in the wood, and on those exhilarating night flights, I was untaught. My experiences and understandings were *sui generis*, so completely my own that I could not conceive that they had meaning, let alone importance, for anyone else at all. Yet this was a dimension in which I continued to grow and to delight. The noonday world, with its rattletrap trams, and the evening world, with its twilight hazes and voices of children going home from play, its sad and pensive lamplit streets, were all too familiar to me. The early morning was almost unknown. For a brief spell of childhood I became an early riser. In 1917 and 1918, when the German blockade was at its height, we were a country near to starving. We were always hungry. I sometimes queued for two hours to get two pounds of rotting, runny potatoes which in happier times would have been regarded as unfit for pigs. To get meat, as well as pocket money, my brother and I went to work for the local butcher every Saturday. His weekend meat used to arrive on Friday nights or early on Saturday mornings. Queues began to form at eight in the morning. The shop would be sold out by eleven. My brother would get there as early as six to help with the sausage-making or the parcelling. I might arrive at seven to begin deliveries on foot, weighed down with an enormous basket, or even two. It was a new solitary experience to slip throught the silent streets at six or half past on a frosty morning, cold but alert, watching a red sun rise over our still wooded hills, and to see on spring mornings how the gliding sun subtly transformed everything from moment to moment, tearing the fragrance from the bowered and scalloped hawthorns, swivelling the west-falling shadows across the bare clean streets where the cats began to scratch and clean themselves and the dogs to roughen and to roll in the dew-sprinkled dust. With joy I was lifted up into the unimaginable purity of that early morning freshness. I saw the world as skilfully recreated each morning by the knives of light, scalpels of the spirit, carving anew now a gable, now a bedroom window with blinds down, now gilding a red chimney pot with a crown of lemon light, or blocking out the tent of shadow let fall by the chestnut tree. The world could have died in my sleep and come into resurrection in all the unfamiliarity of the sun's eastern light as I watched, privileged observer of the first Genesis day. A godlike light: it filled me with delight and awe. How strange was the turning earth, spinning into the sun's light with an undulant bird chorus, wearing its dunce's cap of night. How mysterious the sun and all its planets and the remote dance of incredibly distant heavenly bodies. I had no words: nevertheless, the power and majesty of the universe, beginning with my re-created streets, used to make my pulse beat faster, my cheeks burn, my eyes dance. But if I began to think it out, to ask what it meant — how far away were the sun and the stars, and was infinity something you never really could come to the end of? — then I got vertigo, and to escape the terror of those endless vistas and crushing heights I was glad to rush to the safety of the marrow bones and mutton scrag of the butcher's shop, and to begin, with downcast eyes, lest someone should read therein something I could not bear to be known about me, the tasks which helped to keep us fed

17

during the week. If I were serving at early communion then this was to me the ritual fulfilment of the worship of the Godhead probing the streets outside with needles of silver sharpened on the wheel of night. The sun beat through the stained glass of the window and stretched tight ribbons of blue and green and yellow into the chancel and the nave. The dust motes trembled in them. We were robed in white cottas and albs of stiff unbleached linen; my white girdle was pulled tight round me. In vestments I felt pure and dignified, and justified of God. The few communicants were shadows by the pillars. The low sun through the east window crowned with light the priest's head and bathed my serving hands in its own wine. The service murmured along, the sun rising beyond the window, as if it were God himself ascending above creation to renew a holy world we would have ruined again by nightfall.

4

Puberty came: if this was a transformation of the body, it was also a convulsion of the soul. I had lived the two dimensions, one of the noonday world where everything was assured and the other of a soul life where nothing was, without sense of the contradiction between them. They remained as strictly separate as school and play, indoors and outdoors. Now I felt my restlessness and dissatisfaction increase daily without knowing what it was that so troubled me. I knew what dissatisfied me in my own self. The concept of purity had profound and emotionally-loaded meaning to boys of my generation. Even when they lost it, they longed for their own sense of innocence back again. I thought daily of suicide because I could neither mentally nor physically hold on to my purity, despite the rigorous and even athletic personal life which made my brother and me devotees of cold baths, morning runs, and Sandow's exercises.

My discovery of my own puberty (I did not know the word or comprehend the event) occurred on the most disastrous of days, the June morning on which my little brother was born. I was sent with a letter to the far away doctor we

18

had suddenly adopted (mother had had a tiff with the doctor down the street) and the long journey by foot took me over our fine wooded One Tree Hill. I had made many such trips with messages before and brought back medicine, and thought nothing of this incomprehensible adult activity. I was far too pixilated, but scared too, by the developments of my childhood body to do more than loiter through my own confused preoccupations in the divine June morning.

I returned to find anxious neighbours about the house, scolding me for a lazy, laggard, thoughtless boy. Didn't I understand how urgent it was? How ill my mother was? I understood *now*. My mother, in painful labour, filled the house with her exhausted cries. I was sure that she was dying, and that I was responsible, and fled in guilt and anguish into the back garden and crouched under the rose arbour with my hands over my ears praying to God not to let her die. Even then I did not know why she was ill. Not until much later was I told that I had a new little brother and that my mother was gravely ill and stumbled in my mind to grasp the connection between the two events, a connection it seemed impossible for a boy to make who, so young, understood absolutely nothing of the travail of women in childbirth, though he had some knowledge by then of how babies were begotten.

It is hard for the derisory younger generations today to understand the attitudes of those times towards sex. Yet it is necessary if one is to understand what religion — and for that matter nature — meant to us. And especially to me. I and my contemporaries were both innocent and ignorant. We were innocent because the world seemed to us pure and simple and noonday: we judged the world by our generous childish reaction to it. We did not conceive of hidden things, of concealed perversions and lusts. Nor would we have understood them easily. We thought the world honourable. We were totally ignorant about sex, except that which was whispered along the schoolboy grapevine, because there was a total tabu on the discussion of it (at least in our presence) among adults, and in books and newspapers. I remember that as young scouts we were summoned to a special service for boys and an owlish preacher warned us about great temptations and dangers we could fall into. He was hinting at masturbation,

19

but we understood nothing. On the way home we clustered under street lamps to discuss it. One said he thought it was telling dirty stories and another thought it was going to the pictures too often which damaged your eyes and another ventured that it was going to bed too late. Most argued that it was *smoking*, though there was one quiet child who believed it was something else but wasn't going to say.

It was possible to grow up in a curiously sexless world in that age so unlike our own, and to prove incapable of reading the plain signs under one's nose, like the twelve-year old Leo in L. P. Hartley's *The Go-Between*, who was of our world, after all, not of this, and with one change of letter could have been *Les*.

One could even have a sweetheart and discuss love. I had such a sweetheart, with fair hair and blue eyes who came with me when I took my much-loved little sister out in her pram. Margaret had her pram, with an infant brother, and we were like a solemn married couple talking about our children. I read about love in the romantic novels I pored over — I would read anything — without ever suspecting it had anything to do with sex.

All this is so familiar a tale that one need not pause over it: the novels and biographies of our day document that world with cynical relish. All the same there was a sexual underground in our co-educational school of jokes repeated, Bibles consulted and whispered colloquies between bowed flushed faces in corners.

There was absolutely no adult of my world from whom one dared seek information, so I tried the grapevine. My friend Mickey with whom I walked home boasted he knew everything and I pressed him hard. He put me off with a fantastic cloacal story I was intended not to believe and eventually, reluctantly, told me, without obscenity, what he knew of sexual intercourse. I was silent with unbelief. I knew so little, at eleven, of my own physique. My knowledge of the body of girl or woman was nil. The clothes were all. The fantastic acrobatics of sexual penetration my friend proposed seemed beneath contempt — funny even, were they not in bad taste. After all one's mother and father were being accused of acts beneath all human honour and dignity, as though they were dogs in the street. So I dismissed it all with an airy scorn and perhaps even forgot it. Football was better than that lunatic world, and I drew apart from the grapevine.

The disillusion, a year before puberty, was as traumatic as it could be. It occurred in my military hospital. At that time we had a soldier-patient in my hospital ward who was a music hall artist in peace time — a female impersonator! He was querulous and disagreeable and we did not get on together. On concert nights I was responsible for the distribution of free cigarettes to the men and he was always accusing me of giving the other men more than I gave him. It could have been true, but it strengthened dislike. I had a boy's contempt for small-mindedness.

Of course he boasted about his life on the halls and was pressed by the other patients as he grew better to do his turn at the weekly concert. I was sceptical, but to my astonishment he did appear, hardly recognizable, ogling us all through his make-up, wearing a flaxen wig almost a bee-hive, high heels, false breasts and a tight golden lamé dress like a one-piece sexual uniform into which he had been poured. So armoured, he minced about the stage singing some of the sexy songs of the day and exchanging banter with hooting, cat-calling, excited soldiers. The transformation was so perfect I could not believe my eyes: nor endure his vanity when it was all over.

Later, I made my last rounds before going home in a darkened tram round which shrapnel might be flying. I collected the soldiers' letters and shouted out 'Good night chaps!' Dear God, such dutifulness, conscientiousness, in a twelve-year-old! I went to the upper ward, where the female impersonator had his bed, and said my piece, and a rather sick soldier asked me to empty his bed-bottle. I took his overfull flask, carrying it gingerly, for the urine slopped over my knuckles, to the lavatory to empty it, and wash and return.

I had to pass through the further ward on my delicate journey, and there was the impersonator in his female glory in the middle of excited young soldiers who were pawing at his sheath of golden lamé. They were a little drunk perhaps. Something was going on. Coarsely they were urging one bright-eyed, white-cheeked boy, whom consumption had marked down, to 'finish the job properly an' chuck 'er on the bed'. This boy had his arms around the impersonator and was shuffling his loins against her lamé plated rear.

'Stow it,' said one. 'Ere's scouty.'

'E's alright,' said another, 'don't mind 'im. The kid ain't green.'

But they all stopped and stared at me and the impersonator tittered, and this told everything. I shrank under this cruel, knowing probing, hoping my knees would bear me, and went past them, eyes downcast, bearing the trembling vessel as though it were the chalice for the altar of St Hilda's. I had to return. I had to return past them again. To return. They were still waiting and judging me, a watchful frozen group. I could not look at them.

'You ain't green, are you scouty?'

'Are you, scouty?' asked another. 'I'll bet you ain't. I knew everythink there was to know at your age. And I'd tried my luck.'

This brought a roar of laughter against me. Yet I bore up, and would not collapse. Unspeaking I went past them and down the ward and put the wet urine bottle on the sick soldier's locker and went out of the ward and carefully closed the door. At the top of the tulip stairs I crumpled up in a faint. I came to, fearful of being discovered in that state, and crawled down the circular stairs with a swimming head, and out in the courtyard I vomited under the pear tree.

Mickey was proved to be right. What was hinted at, in the shape of perversity, made it unhappily possible to accept the sexual gymnastics he had described. The infamous had made normal sex quite clear. More, the attitude of the soldiers confronted me with the gigantic grown-up sexual conspiracy, to which it was leeringly suggested I must already belong, had long belonged, and that anything to the contrary in my eyes or bearing was a boy's sly deceit.

My mother saw my distress though I tried to hide it from her eyes and questions. She discovered that I was ill and had a temperature, and I could only say that I had been sick. I was sent to bed with a glass of hot milk and spent the next day playing with my toy soldiers in the hills and valleys of the counterpane, trying to get back to a wholeness of mind I had for ever lost. The sense of the rectitude of the world has disappeared. It was not to be trusted. That the horror of the halfpenny history book was present in the world I had come to accept, though I tried to hide from it. Now the horror had invaded me. When I saw a grossly pregnant woman get on a tram, and recognized her condition, I nearly fainted.

I found my restlessness and unhappiness increase daily without knowing always what it was that troubled me. But after that June day on which my mother nearly died I knew what dissatisfied me in my own self. As I said, the concept of purity had profound and emotionally loaded meanings to boys of my generation: this I know because two of my friends wanted to commit suicide because of the burden of masturbation. I too. I was going to leave my clothes on a solitary beach and swim out till I drowned. Even if only half-intended, it was a serious protest.

Today, of course, there are textbooks for children which commend masturbation and instructional films which demonstrate it. These fatuous specimens of the pullulating media say that the boys of my time were frightened to death by the propaganda against masturbation which threatened its addicts with insanity, venereal disease, tuberculosis, spinal weakness, pimples and so on. These genuine Victorian fears were never spelt out to us — rather they drifted through the grapevine or could be sifted out of an occasional pamphlet or book. We could be momentarily frightened, but soon recovered. We did not think we were going to die because of it. But we condemned ourselves because of it.

What seriously worried us was the moral issue: what we were doing was against our sense of honour. It was dishonourable because it had to be furtive, solitary, concealed, denied. It could not be part of a life lived in the open, before all men, which was part of our boyish dream: impure, certainly, because it was always accompanied by the most fearful and immoral lust and imaginings. We were quite capable of recognizing our own sexual evil. A life of religion and prayer seemed the only armour against surrender. And this is the difference between that age and ours, that we recognized sexual evil and fought it in our own appetites and lusts. If we were not always capable of distinguishing it from sexual good, that was our naiveté and ignorance which this age is entitled to mock. But we did understand obsession, which this age

23

approves. I felt suffocated by my obsessions as boy and youth: they made the cage one was living in so small: no matter what satisfactions I obtained or how, my mind rattled round and round the sexual squirrel-run without finding a way out. And how could we win when our heroes were against us? Ernest Thompson Seton in his *The Book of Woodcraft and Indian Love* wrote, 'Rest assured of this, more nations have been wiped out by sex abuse than by bloody war.' And even John Hargrave, who ought to have known better, published in his *The Great War Brings It Home* his own sketch of a pine tree hacked by an axe with the sap dribbling from it. His comment in the text was that the abuse of the racial organs drained away the life-blood or the 'vital force' of body and mind. I was too young even to conceive that they too might be trapped in the brutal myths of the age. They were the exemplars who could not be questioned!

There had to be a way out. I remember telling myself as an adolescent that there must be other things worth doing and thinking about — sport, swimming, scouts, poetry, God — and that obsessed with sex all day and night one would just die: it was a sort of madness. Today I would say, yes, that is true, and that as a boy I recognized its demonic character. I saw religion as a necessary answer. It gave a dimension to life which was not sexual. It offered the loving support of God in what was otherwise one's incommunicable misery. It proffered a discipline and a dedication. Just by its own existence and by the glory I had already experienced in so many ways it said that sex was not all, there were other goals and by seeking them one enlarged a life threatened otherwise with contraction to a single phallic point. I had not yet heard of sublimation, a word now used pejoratively to mean a false alternative to sex. But the word is unimportant compared with the fact that no human society has ever been content with pure vassalage to sex but has sought social restraints and religious sanctions against its potential ubiquity and power. So I may take comfort; my small self was fighting the battle humanity has always fought. Alas, my armour was puny then.

Despite church, things got to such a pitch that I began to prepare for suicide. I happened, when playing in the country with my friend Osbert Walter, to bat a lump of wood over the gorse bushes and into a road where it hit a cyclist who promptly fell off and tore his trousers. A silent screen episode, really. He caught hold of me like an aggrieved Buster Keaton and worked up that comedian's capacity for righteous but misplaced indignation. Verbally bullying me, he took my name and address, and thereafter I received weekly letters threatening legal proceedings unless I paid for a new pair, the cost of which would be ten shillings. It was with difficulty those days that I mustered a shilling. It was only in later years that I began to wonder whether my persecutor had been poor too, and the damage to his trousers a disaster not altogether comic. Yet he also enjoyed threatening me: so much was clear. I could never tell my parents anything just then, so convinced was I of my own complete worthlessness and of their inability to help (they were poor anyway) but I plucked up courage to write to the Chief Scout, Sir Robert Baden-Powell, about this new disaster, and my masturbation, and how I prayed and prayed daily but no help came.

Back came a letter beautifully typed, full of good advice about daily cold baths (which I already took) and not eating pickles and not praying too much and getting obsessed (though he did not use the word). In a neat paragraph he skittled the claim of my Buster Keaton cyclist for a new pair of trousers at my expense. It calmed me and braced me. It was a well-meaning letter from a very kindly old man. It is obvious to me now that he must have taken enormous pains with it. I am sorry I did not keep it. I did not try suicide. It began to seem absurd to die for (among other things) a pair of flannel trousers. In any case I had no money to get to the coast. And if I had had the money, I thought shrewdly, it would still cost me less to pay for the trousers than to drown.

In sex probably I went through no more than any other sensitive and honourable boy, but I surpassed all, I think, in my fear of losing my relationship with the world and with the power that burned and flamed beyond it. A tremulous uncertainty developed in me about the noonday world. What sustained it? What held it together?

A tall building could fall, a horse run away, a house catch fire, a bridge collapse. As a little boy all disasters, such as the tram which turned over at the points at the bottom of the road, all consequences of war or accident, were welcome as entertaining exceptions to the dull durability of objects in the midday light. One wanted the world to be more exciting, less sterile and futile.

5

Now I saw all things, people as well, as fragile, vulnerable, perishable —

> Change and decay in all around I see,
> O thou who changest not,
> Abide with me.

as one day I was to find A. N. Whitehead had seen them too. Ashamed and anxious I hunted my parents' faces for signs of age. Looking at the facial creases and folds and worn eyes of my grandmother, and the sadness of her expression in repose, I was struck a physical blow on the heart with the thought, 'she will die soon.' It was unbearable that anyone could look so forsaken.

I was discovering the necessity of death within myself and others, and the impermanency of the works of human hands too. It affected my daily life. If *things* had to come to an end, why not at the moment my steps reached them? Would the spire fall as I passed it, or the tram overturn, or the bridge collapse under the weight of the train? My walk to school became a timid scutter from one island of safety to another, even from one side of the road to another, to avoid the menaces of existence. Happily, once at school or with friends I forgot my fears.

When the war ended, camping became possible again. My first experiences were with the Scouts, but these were not audacious enough for me, and I planned expeditions far and wide, testing myself and my resolution and my skill. They had to be on foot. There was no money for bikes. Indeed we had almost no equipment at all, everything had to be improvized. A friend, Les Bowles, and I made an expedition to St Leonard's Forest, walking the last ten miles (we had no more money) from Three Bridges, carrying all our belongings on poles between us. There we bivouacked under great pines by

26

a spring at the forest's edge, and setting ourselves a regime of training, began every day with a mile run and a cold bathe. It was in a horse trough and presently the horses objected.

It was a time of gales. The wind, dormant during the day, would rise at night. Lying awake I would hear the gusts get up a mile away and roar through the funnel of our forest valley with the tumult of assaulting battalions. I could trace each furious wave until it broke on the crests of the pine trees above us and passed on out of hearing. A few drops pattered on our flimsy tent, but its walls hardly even stirred, so sheltered and still was it on the forest floor. A Miltonic battle of the heavens, the storm had every nerve in me tense and excited. I willed the boom and suck of every wave to be more violent and tremendous, even though the result would have been disastrous for us. I imagined it as Jehovah's raging, as the Lord of Hosts storming with his invincible armies, or else as the passage of spirits of death and destruction over a passover world. It was not possible to think of this drama as impersonal, as merely the common air at high speed, certainly not to one who had already listened dumb with fear to the air bombardments of enemy planes. Like a storm at sea it had malice and intention. After such a night I would crawl out of my tent expecting that the hand of the Lord had stripped the forests bare. No such thing. The wind had played on every tree in the valley as though on an organ, drawing from the forest a symphony of its own, exaggerating its own power. Nothing had been destroyed, except for a few twigs whipped down. The air was fresh, limpid, chill, the light altogether new and childlike in its innocence, convicting me of error, as though I had projected on the world the storm of my own being, and true it was that the wind had played upon me, vibrating every nerve as though it were a twig upon a tree. The sense of union with, participation with, nature, the experience already sealed in me, was that which I most ardently, obscurely sought. It drove me to camp in the bitterest weather, barelegged, thigh-deep in November mud in Epping Forest, or to do forced marches in snow and frost and to long for the sting of hail and rain on my bare head. Of course, there was a toughness to be almost inarticulately tested, but there was an identity to be discovered, a self to be forged. In what I thought of as the closest union with nature

27

my life took on meaning: with the whip of the wind through me, the feel of a tree's bark under my fingers, or the smell of grass in my nostrils, I came alive, with a secret exaltation, a joy so penetrating that if it came to me in town where I was seated or still, its exhilaration was too much to bear. I was forced to jump up and move about, or if in bed to dress and go out for a tramp.

Thus began for me tremendous evening or night walks to places which had become as sacred for me as the groves in Attica to Athenians — the hilltop tree, overlooking London, a bank below some hawthorns in Whitefoot Lane, and a tumulus on the hills of Seven Fields, from which the whole span of crackling stars rose derisively like an alternative universe above the hurtling planet. I would throw myself on the grass and press my cheek to it. The delicate hiss of wind in the grass was the trickling away of time. I hardly used the word prayer to myself, but it was prayer. I sought to be utterly still and to will myself into the being of the grass or of the soil which gritted in my fingernails and beneath these, of the whole earth bearing me effortlessly up, swinging me over as it went gyrating in the dance for which heavenly bodies called the tune. It was so unspeakably strange that I should be alive and should be 'I', and should seek, face downwards and alone, on this hill, to penetrate into the being of the earth on which I lived, and without which my own being was inconceivable. Yet how could I penetrate something whose being was so alien and remote from me? It does not feel, it will not feel, I cried. I longed, trembled, to be part of that being, to possess it, inseparably. Only in death would it be inalienably mine, but then because it would possess me, its obduracy would have outwilled, outworn me. The sense of personal fragility and impotence was even greater if I turned over and stared at the watching stars. What could my life mean against that immensity? Yet all the time I had the sense, and sought to deepen the sense, of that which burned and rolled through the baffling world, the light which shone through a glass darkly, but through a glass not evenly dark so that moments came when the flash blinded me, and I went rigid, fearful and joyful in anticipation, hardly daring to breathe. 'God,' I used to pray, clenching my fists. 'God. God. God,' till the word became meaningless. Or 'Please,' or 'No, no, no!' Then jump up, walking quickly, running, lest I threshed about like a madman in an incomprehensible anguish. It was just such an excursion that took me, full of my secret joy, to that tree on the hilltop to pray with the wind in my face, on the night when everything was dissolved into that wild, unsummoned grief for all men, a grief never to be forgotten throughout a long, busy life.

6

One looks back anxiously, sorrowfully, on that adolescence, and with a little dread at the clinical phrases which might so neatly dissect and dismiss it. How easy to see a boy in that portrait who was a loner, antisocial, full of unsatisfied sex and bad conscience, perhaps rootless too. How wrong it would be, even had all those judgements been true of me, and at some moments all might have been, I suppose. Yet the true effect of all those experiences of expanding life of the spirit was glory, a joy in the world which was heightened even in that suffering to which, as a child, one saw no end.

I was born in Dublin, by pure accident, for my father worked on the business side of newspapers and had taken on the job of circulation manager of the *Irish Independent*. Sounds grand, but I imagine it was underpaid for he did not stay long. There was no future in it.

I was born in that fabled land not far from Dun Laoghaire
Where the railway runs straight with canal and raw of bone
   boys
Make shiny the bridge parapets and fish or fortunes hook
In litter and emerald ooze.
A modest red house with yellow lace curtains
At the corner of May Street. My father, brown-eyed and
   yearning
With elegant English moustaches walked the sharp Dublin
   mornings.
To the newspaper building by Sackville Street bridge over
   Liffey.

Reserved among strangers, with looks of disdain hiding
  singular fears,
Saw the meetings, the Fenian banners, the Phoenix Park
  murders,
'A terrible beauty is born'.

But sadly, for I would have enjoyed becoming an Anglo-
Irish intellectual, I was not to be tied to an Irish destiny. My
father was restless with ambition and we were whisked away
before I was even old enough to realize that for my mother
Ireland consisted of just two insuperable scourges — ubiquitous fleas and stewed tea. She was glad to see the back of
them. She had only one compliment — the Irish spoke beautiful English. We went to Newcastle-upon-Tyne and then to
Sheffield, where I first went to council school and learnt to
toboggan down icy roads. On my last visit to Hunters' Bar
I discovered that the school was still there, grey, rocklike and
rugged, built to last the ages, unchanged except for the
addition of a dining hall. Four years old, I peed in the snow
on the day of my enrolment (it always seemed to be snowing
in Sheffield) and was hauled before the class and told off.
But I did not know what a 'class' was, nor why this strange
huge-busted woman in black had assumed a god-like authority over me, nor even what my offence had been. I burst into
tears. My chagrin was the worse for my pleasure had been in
scientific discovery that the snow turned first yellow then
greeny-blue. And it steamed!
My mother and father came from Leeds and there all our
relations lived, so it is a little astonishing that none of the
children managed to be born there. Mother and father had
both been brought up in the famous back-to-backs and
father's home cul-de-sac as a child had been so narrow and
traffic-free in the evening that he was able to tie a string from
one door knocker to another *across the street*, and with one
brisk tap bring two irate ladies simultaneously to their
(mostly unused) front doors where, as likely as not, they
would find when they went to untie the string that the
knocker had been given a lick of treacle. My paternal grandfather was a brushmaker and my grandmother never forgave
him for dying and leaving her a widow dependent on ungrate-
ful and restless children. I cannot imagine what the life of a

brushmaker could have been in grimy nineteenth-century Leeds except that it meant that my father left school at twelve to become a printer's devil on a local newspaper and taught himself shorthand to earn a bob or two reporting football matches and was wild enough to lark about in graveyards at night, frightening the girls.

My maternal grandfather was quite a figure. He was the first sanitary inspector appointed by the Leeds Corporation, earned a pound a week, and had his name printed on the top of the official notepaper. He wore a suit and went to church in a top hat and was slight and fragile and elegant. He was a success, and, as the sociologists would say today, 'upwardly mobile', except that he and my grandmother never lived long enough to enjoy it all over again in their children and grandchildren. I regret that I never met this grandfather, for, judging by the merriness and eccentricity of his children, he must have been quite a man. But I have his photograph and many letters in his immaculate copper plate complaining of his son Arthur's behaviour on the rampage in the United States without benefit of money, sense or overmuch literacy. Arthur was the 'bottle-fed' Uncle Herbert of *The Boy Down Kitchener Street* who once sat down on my slice of bread and treacle and told us the most marvellous stories of his adventures. All untrue. And so a boyhood hero, with the most highly polished boots in London. We said, 'He's on Poplar Council' or 'He's something on the council.' Off duty, he looked it. My mother disapproved of her brother, but whether for telling those outrageous lies about himself or for being a dustman, I never knew. And as for floridly beautiful Auntie Florrie, seduced by a sadistic bath attendant in her teens who threatened her with death if she did not submit sexually, then divorced and married to a tall thin Canadian soldier, and medium and founder of a spiritualist church in Los Angeles, what am I to say of her? She was an original indeed. She turns up as the fabulous Auntie Blossom in *The Boy Down Kitchener Street*. I was once, in 1947, sunning myself on the foredeck of a cross-channel steamer and got into conversation with a young American couple. It turned out that they came from Los Angeles. 'Oh,' I said, in the fatuous way one does, 'I have an aunt living there — she runs a church. Mrs Hall?'

'Mrs *Florence* Hall?' the man asked.

'Yes, certainly. Mrs Florence Hall. My Aunt Florrie.'
There was a dumbfounded silence.
'*The* Mrs Florence Hall?'
My opinion of my eccentric auntie went up by leaps and bounds. But she was as accident prone as the rest of us and ended her life rather poor in a downtown hotel in Vancouver. She had no children and in her later years wrote us rather downcast letters to which we did not always reply. Her thin Canadian, gassed at the Somme, and saved from a German bullet by an issue New Testament in his breast pocket, had died, and she was alone and old, and felt that God had deserted her and there was nothing left to live for. Still she had long outlived my mother, who had died, speech and memory gone, a wizened thing, from cerebral arterio-sclerosis in an Epsom asylum in the week of the invasion of Normandy, with her family scattered by war and far from her, and fifteen years after my father who when only fifty had killed himself with whisky. Yes, accident prone, my father.

The little half-timer practising shorthand with fingers stained with printers' ink never knew what hit him in Fleet Street, to which he gravitated as London Manager of the newly founded *Southern Daily Post* in 1910 or 1911, coming to live with his growing family in a big respectable house in Forest Hill at £5 a quarter rent! But the paper's first issue coincided with a rail strike and railways were then the only means of distribution over a wide area. The strike lasted three weeks and killed the new paper and my father was out of a job. By the time he was on his feet again the war came and ruined him, and presently he had five children. It was a struggle to get restarted after the Great War: then he had a ten-year run at the top in Fleet Street, but he lost the two papers on which we lived — *The Cambria Daily Leader* and *The Grimsby Daily Telegraph* — through the amalgamations of 1929 and 1930, and was shortly dead from alcoholism. I, who had been his assistant for some years, had left him — deserted him, because I could not bear to see his deterioration — for freelance journalism which proved disastrous, and a prison too, because one could not escape from it back into a regular job during the depression. I was stuck in a no-man's land until I took up teaching, and thought often of suicide. Accident prone too, you see. The accidents of the fathers are visited on the sons.

My brother Kenneth, my sister Marjorie and I were sent to a Central School after the 11 plus. A Central School was a place where they gave you an education to fit you for an office. Why not to a grammar school? There was no money and only a few free places and we all failed to qualify. It was ridiculous, of course. When Kenneth sat the Junior Civil Service exam a few years later he came twelfth in the whole country and top in French, and we were all of that calibre too. He put down his name for the Foreign Office but they sent him to be an office boy in the Post Office. Boys from his class were not expected to aspire so high. When I was fourteen a group of us went to our form mistress and asked about matriculation, of which we had just heard forbidding accounts, and universities, of which we knew nothing at all. 'Oh,' came the shocked reply, 'universities are not for boys like you.' Indeed, she was right. Universities were still a class privilege in the twenties. We were the poor kids. I did not set foot in universities until I came to teach in them.

It is one thing to be socially 'upwardly mobile' as my maternal grandfather and my own father were, but it is another thing to catch up culturally. That takes longer. So though there were books about in my boyhood and we all read indiscriminately, there was not much talk of writers beyond Dickens and Scott and the lady who wrote *The Lamplighter*, and nothing at all about music and poetry or the arts. But there was much discussion about the music hall, since many of my cousins lived by it, and a hard, sweaty, insecure racket it was. My cousins Belle and Frank toured with the stage names Terry and Yorke as 'The Comedy Tap-Dance Duo'. This link brought us the friendship of the manager of the London Palladium and so an extensive part of my education was to sit in a free seat in the front row of the stalls on Monday nights, chewing Russian toffees, and waiting for the comics. It was strange that I became a writer, for the music hall insisted that all poets, painters and musicians were quite mad, dressing incredibly, incoherent in speech, fanatic in behaviour and unsuccessful with the girls. It was quite a shock to meet my first poet, whose name I have forgotten, who presented me with a prize for elocution, and to find that he was tweedy and pipe-smoking and rather ordinary.

33

And so it came about that I left school just before my sixteenth birthday and went to work as a junior clerk at Kearley and Tonge's in Aldgate. They were wholesale grocers and owned the International Tea Company's Stores. Everything was now to do by myself, through evening classes and youth movements, through reading and politics. Father was no use. For all his kindness of heart and his loneliness, he drove his children away by his reticence and self-effacement. It gave him the air of walking away from our troubles and interests. Perhaps indeed our enthusiasms bored him: they were naive, argumentative, noisy: he had no interest in ideas, ideologies, only in 'getting on'. I wish I had known him better for it was only in later years that I have come to understand what a strain it must have been to be so ambitious, so upwardly mobile and so insecure in himself and in his posts. Climbing out of the brushmaker class, escaping his angry and dominant mother who ruled her children with a rod of iron (a little brother ran away and was lost for ever), must have taken a lot of strength, and left him anxious and exhausted too. He deserved to have landed up somewhere less dangerous, less boozy, less competitive than the feverish Fleet Street of his day. For he was at once ambitious and disdainful of conflict and in-fighting. He was in a way *too* honourable for his world, too intent on being a superior person, and without the inner confidence to face disaster, and without education. I am sure the big business manipulations which lost him his two papers increased his guilt feelings, and in some inner torment he blamed his own inadequacies. I can only guess at the heart of this elegant and dapper little man who came to die at fifty. It was a cruel fate after so much striving. When I wrote *Periwake* (the novel which the *News Chronicle* called 'Mr Polly brought down to earth') it was of a doomed little man like my father that I was thinking. I had often found him unconscious from drink on the front doorstep, when, grown up, I came home from meetings late at night. There must have been much of my father in me, I now see. The terrible illness which brought me down in my late twenties was born of too much striving and too much anxiety. But it did not quite kill me.

In the thirties, campaigning for my youth movement, I visited my father's older brother Jim in Chadderton,

Lancashire, and stayed the night. In so doing I stepped back into the nineteenth century, into the world my father had struggled from and from which his little brother had simply bolted. Uncle's one-storied worker's cottage stood in a terrace in a cobbled street. One stepped straight out of the street into his living room. His cottage was hardly more than this one room with the kitchen range for cooking and heating and a curtained bed recess for man and wife. There was a tiny scullery, still lit only by a gas jet, and a small separate child's bedroom. There was no bathroom. The W.C. was outside. It was November. My uncle and aunt retired for the night to the child's bedroom. The one child had grown up. I was left to the bed recess.

Early next morning I was woken by the sound of the knocker-up clattering on the cobbles through the dank November mist and tapping on doors or clanking his pole against windows. Sometimes he was answered with a cheery shout: often with silence: but presently there were morning sounds — the rasp of coal being shovelled from outhouses, the clanking of metal dustbin lids. Doors slammed. I could hear the newspaper boy running, coughing and snivelling, through the cold. A paper slammed through the letter box not far from me. Presently the mill sirens went and a strange sound came from the street, drowning everything else. It was like the drumming of a downpour of rain and the slurring and slushing of a torrent of water. I believed it was a flood and went across the now cold hearth to draw the curtains and look out.

It was a flood, a human one, of mill girls in their wooden clogs along the cobbled streets. Mill girls in dark clothes, with black shawls drawn over their heads and wrapped around their small tender bosoms. Young girls with pale drawn morning faces in the cold: hurrying to work from tea and porridge eaten beside still cold hearths. It was the clatter of their countless clogs on the cobbles polished by rain and feet that produced the unforgettable sound of drumming rain and rushing flood. Lowry people. The industrial revolution made real. Presently the sound as magically ceased. Only the running laggards were left.

I watched them all pass — swaying and fluttering along, graceful and ghostly, anxious and doomed in the November

35

dawn, and saw at once the world from which my father, not long dead, had escaped. The eldest son of my brushmaker grandfather, my Uncle Jim had become a bookbinder and so followed a craft like his father. He had the pride and independence of the craftsmen of those days: a contented man. When the war came and my *Annihilation of Man* was a great success, he bound and tooled a copy for me in blue and gold, and, impeccable, it stands on the shelf that holds the red and gold leatherbound library copies of the rest of my writings. From my father I inherited nothing but an already worn electroplate cruet set presented by his colleagues on the *Sheffield Independent* just before he left for London.

Perhaps my father would have been happier if he had settled for bookbinding too and stayed with the pale, saucy mill girls and become president of the Oddfellows.

7

However, if in my teenage I had much of my father in me, there was also what I inherited from mother to be reckoned with. I was as full as he was of fear and insecurity, and convinced like him (however well disguised) of my own unworthiness, and I shared with him that sadness before the world which I often glimpsed in his brilliant, neuropathic brown eyes.

My mother was an extrovert and less complicated. She was a doer, and an overdoer: to sit down during the day and take a nap or read the newspaper was quite beyond her while there was work to be done. Everything was subordinated to the 'work-pattern' she had formed in her mind about the day or days ahead. She had no apparent consciousness of the need for leisure. Evensong on Sundays, and holidays at the seaside, uncomfortably wedged on the hard Eastbourne pebbles in a corner, out of the wind, reading the *Express* or the *Mirror* and munching ginger biscuits gone soft from exposure to the salt air, and minding our clothes while we bathed, and exclaiming 'Never!' or 'I'd shoot them!' over the morning's headlined tragedies — these alone constituted her leisure. All that she excitedly did for our great feasts and enormous parties must count as work, I am afraid. But then work was her life.

She was not unlettered or unread. After all, she had, a bright, beautiful young girl, trained as a nurse. But she was curiously innocent and unworldly, hating gossip and always believing good of people out of her own instinctive goodness. She detested disturbing ideas or theories. Her very bright zeal had given her a tremendous sense of drama and she would recount the incidents of her limited day so enthrallingly that our own lives were heightened by it. One saw in that girl what distinguished Auntie Florrie and Uncle Arthur, who both dramatized their lives.

And so with my mother's genes, too, rattling about inside me, and with her example constantly before me, I could not be idle or self-pitying. I had to be a doer too, or life would have no meaning. From my mother one learnt that it was *dishonourable* not to be a doer: it was for that reason that my first childish poem was about duty.

Doing was the thing, preferably with friends, and I was blessed with staunch friends. Long night walks with them, or weekends camping, were my university, in which everything was thrashed out, including the Sufi mysticism precociously practised by my friend Osbert Walter. Such nonsense! His family was a stage family and he was even better at filling his life with fantasy than I was. I never abandoned my friends for a lonely walk on my own. Indeed as a very little boy I was fanatically public spirited, spending most of my precious spare time after school in air raids and fog and cold running messages for wounded soldiers in Lewisham Military Hospital, buying their stamps and cigarettes and fish and chips, despite the kind of disaster I have already described. I was shocked to find on getting into my winter overcoat one October that it smelt rancid with the fish and chip parcels of the previous winter.

I soothed these troubled and sometimes dying soldiers, translated the bawdy letters they received from girls in France, emptied their bed bottles, served their meals and in off-times wound bandages in the staff room, all out of a sense of patriotic duty. Sometimes the wounded men broke down, sometimes they told me they knew they were dying. Occasionally a soldier went mad. Yet, despite my own fears of death

37

and madness, I faced it all with an odd, steely maturity. A strange boy.

I was not even specially egocentric. The moral world of my mother disapproved not only of boasting but even of talking about oneself. It was selfishness. One was expected to write one's triumphs and illnesses down. It was not good taste to suffer. Indeed, I have carried all through my life, and still cannot shed, the absurd obsession that illness is a moral as well as a physical failure. I am certain my mother thought that people *ought not* to be ill and catching this notion from her, I applied it to myself, but oddly never to the wounded soldiers.

The stoicism I now detect in my teenage self made me most loyal and disciplined in the movements I joined. Almost immediately I worked my way up to leadership and presently, still in my teens, founded my own youth movement. Even in my livelihood I was not without modest achievement, becoming a full-time editor at the age of seventeen. I was certainly not an antisocial failure, but, measured by what my friends were doing, even in a limited, precocious way a success.

Was I happy? I do not think I asked myself that question in those years. I do not think I imagined then that I existed in order to be happy. But to suffer, yes. Poets suffered. Even bad poets. Therefore to suffer was some proof of identity and purpose and perversely an occasion for happiness. But had I been all that is clinically required by way of diagnosis, not every such boy sees God burning in the windblown bushes.

I was not, even then, a pre-Freudian young man, but a post-Freudian. Not yet sixteen, I had struggled through Mac-Dougall's *Psychology* in the Home University Library (which I had bought together with F. A. Servanté's *Psychology of the Boy*) and read articles in *John O' London's, The Nation* and other reviews. I knew already the terrible sentence passed upon my world by those Freudian words of judgement: censor, repression, Oedipus complex, compensation, sublimation, neurosis; which rendered every emotion suspect and convicted almost every life of being lived in bad faith. I looked initially for the symptoms in myself and my friends, poisoning soon the wells of love itself by my readiness to swallow them whole. I paid attention particularly, in view of all that was said even then in psychological hostility to God and religious experience (as projected self or sublimated sex or father fear), to my own faith and my deepest most private soul-life. I could see indeed that theoretically Freud could be right if one could accept that everything flowed from the inside to the outside. But what indeed if the glory after all was outside and shining in, and the word spoken in the ear was not a voice in the head? Then the Freudians were demeaning the godly tumult, which swept my world like the forest wind and was the source of its majesty and movement, into some shabby self-deception. Even at sixteen I could see that so intensive a subjectivity destroyed literally everything. If man were all, then God and the world were nothing: man existed, a vacuum in a vacuum. Even at sixteen I knew the meaning of solipsism. If presently I lost my faith it was not for Freudian or other psychological reasons, or even because I judged my experiences to be false or unreal, but because I could no longer accept with a childish simplicity my still childish Christianity. I could not *believe*.

At school and in the Scouts no one bothered to attack the Church, or Christianity: or to defend them. They were accepted for what they were by all of us — a tedious necessity. We had to have a religion. There was a God, of course. Only, the details were all a bore. When I began working, and making new friends from new backgrounds, and joining movements like John Hargrave's Kibbo Kift Kindred, I was thunderstruck to discover Christianity constantly under attack for every conceivable and inconceivable reason. One was somehow under *social* condemnation for believing: it was not done. I discovered how little I knew about my faith and how inept I was at defending it, though I tried.

When I left school — just before my sixteenth birthday — I went to work, as I have said, at Kearley and Tonge's in Mitre Square in the East End of the City. It was not my first choice. I had scaled down my expectations after having failed to get into a bank, British Petroleum, the Savoy Hotel and the Merchant Navy! I worked as a junior clerk in the share department and there was a broad polished mahogany counter under the windows facing the sunny square on which we flung the gigantic red share ledgers. We lolled over it when

39

we had nothing to do, to watch the comings and goings in the square — the drays with their gigantic horses backing into the loading bay, the colourful East Enders moving through the passage by the synagogue, where Jack the Ripper had disembowelled his victims.

Our boss, a friendly young man called Wilson, used to come in at slack times and vault on to the counter and sit cross-legged like a tailor and banter with us.

He discovered that I was religious.

'Not really, Paul?' he said, only half-interested, with a brilliant amused smile at the girls. He was ready to hook the office boy and play him like a fish to amuse them.

'Why shouldn't he be if he wants to be?' said beautiful Miss Franklin opening her great brown eyes.

'How can you be Paul? All that nonsense about Jonah and the whale. Bit fishy if you ask me.' He laughed at his own joke. 'Or Joshua making the sun stand still. How can you, I ask you? Beats me.'

There were many variations on this theme, some as pertinent as the resurrection of the deliquescing Lazarus. I had never thought of religious stories before as having much bearing on what Wilson called 'being religious'. He was attacking something I had never seriously thought of defending. So now I was silent, puzzled, aware too that he was showing off.

The attacks of sophisticated elder people did not entirely pass right over my head. I noted them down 'for further consideration' as we wrote on our files. They just did not seem relevant to my religious experience, which was no longer a church-going one in any serious way. Once I had gone to work I had stopped serving at early communion. I cared little for what Wilson thought or felt, and even enjoyed the gaiety of his polemics, though vulgarian attacks — bleedin' Jesus and such — distressed me. Religion, even if in error, was hardly music hall.

I spoke scathingly of Wilson's scoffing to my friend Osbert Walter. We had been through everything together. We were walking on Sunday, in our best, through the country ravished by the new building. We passed through gaps in torn hedges and walked delicately along planks crossing foundation trenches, and sometimes climbed ladders to unfinished upper storeys in an aimless curiosity. The exposed earth and the piles of bricks had a curious sour smell. Nettles flourished and humps of washed gravel stood around and the scars of lorry wheels criss-crossed the sweet turf. It was saddening.

'Well,' he said, pushing my question away from him crossly with an abrupt movement of rejection. 'Why ask me? Make up your own mind.'

I stopped, shocked and let down, for it was immediately plain from his supercilious tone that he agreed with Wilson. His silhouette was plump against the turquoise sky. He seemed so anxious not to give me pain that he clearly felt guilty.

'Well,' he said, at my savage look, 'Miracles are a tall order, anyway, old man.'

Wilson I did not mind. He was an adult and adults could believe what they liked. They did not count. But Walter was my friend, and this was treachery. It shook the foundations.

'Don't you believe in God then?' I asked fiercely, trembling with the same fear and rage I should have felt if in the war he had announced himself pro-German. 'You must believe in God.'

'Well, it's not exactly that, old man. It's just that miracles are a bit of a facer, after all there are certain facts to be got over. Oh, I believe in God all right.'

'Only you don't believe he can make a little miracle or two. That's not believing.'

'Well, if you have to put it that way, where's the proof he ever does anything like that?'

'Well!' I said, so angry I could have hit him. I turned and ran from him among the unfinished buildings and piles of builders' gravel. He followed me, full of desire to soothe me, his plump face sweating anxiously. He was afraid of my rages.

'Well, no need to get upset, old man. No need to go off the deep end. I only said what I think and really God's a matter of ethics. There's not the least need to get your rag out.'

'You must believe in God, you must, you rotter,' was all I could reply. (We really did talk in the *Gem* and *Magnet* manner.) I would not accept his assurances that you could believe with reservations. It was as good as not believing at all, I cried out. And if you did not believe, what meaning, what possible meaning could life hold? The fool hath said in his heart, 'There is no God!'

Walter's defection hurt and troubled me — by its casualness above all; as though, as with Wilson, belief or unbelief were unimportant, and this I could not accept. And that he could have come to this view without my finding out before, bewildered me. Yet I was afraid he might affect me and I cease to believe too, and disbelief loomed up not as an act of choosing the true from two opinions and discarding the untrue, but as an illness of the mind from which at night I prayed to be spared.

We walked home through wet fields and over rotting stubble, and aimlessly through the builder's wasteland again, unable to talk; we had become estranged. It was a painful and memorable walk.

Outside my house, under the street lamp which poked its glass lantern into the broad leaves of the plane tree, we stopped. Walter lit a cigarette.

'The important thing about religion is not to get emotional,' he said in cold repulse. 'To look at it for its ethics, not its superstitions.'

I was angrily silent, studying the pattern on the bole of the plane tree.

'For instance, you want to read about Sufi'ism, Les, old man, like me. If you like, I'll lend you a book. Christianity is only one of many religions.'

He was as puffed-up as a cockatoo about Sufi'ism and I hated him for it.

I did not answer. In the end, however, it was the opinions of the contemporaries, passing through the same struggles in the same bitter class-torn postwar world, which moved me and won me over. I had, as a boy even, a great respect for clear ideas, a fear of confusion. From friends I learnt socialist and evolutionary ideas and both seemed logical and irrefutable. I could only offer a Christianity barren of explanations — a faith without theology, structureless. How could I reject what seemed true, honest, open in modern ideas and modern science for that confusion? The end could be foreseen.

Yet, intellectually appealing though these anti-religious arguments were, they still stood at a distance from me, like goods behind a shop window one was thinking of buying.

They were in the same world, but I did not yet possess them. I took a long time to make up my mind to buy. My friend Peake used to talk of personal experiences of black and white magic as we walked the wet streets of London after office hours. He would push his hands deep into his pockets and thrust his unhappy face forward, peering short-sightedly at the dusk illuminated like a fair-ground, as if to see the supernatural pinned there for all to read. He had nodded understandingly when I mentioned Wilson's attacks and I thought to myself, 'Here is a man who understands what it is to believe,' and was myself strengthened.

We stood at the corner of Houndsditch one night in August when the British Association for the Advancement of Science was meeting. Bishopsgate was marbled with rain and the home-going city people moved in a ceaseless stream along it, hurrying purposefully under umbrellas like black tulips as if their lives depended upon arriving. Breasting the flood the newsboy stood with a yellow *Star* poster flapping wetly against his knees. 'S. . . denies the Soul,' it said.

I smiled at the poster, confident at that moment in God.

'Fancy anyone saying there is no soul,' I said, 'Silly. Idiotic.'

Peake cocked his massive head to one side and pursed his lips with a smile that betokened private information about the universe.

'Not necessarily silly,' he said. 'By no means. It all depends, but I wouldn't say *silly*.'

He looked at me generously, full of an especial friendliness, willing to make allowances, holding back a certain eagerness to help me, to point out where I was wrong. All this warmth did not dissipate the darkness which began to surround me now that I saw that he, too, did not believe in God. The tide of my unhappiness, usually extinguished while with him, began to rise again. I was desperate about sex, and because its cinematograph performed unceasingly in my head, had made a private vow never to marry, for I should never be worthy. My job made me unhappy when I thought about it — which was often. I was agitated by the fear that life had nothing more to offer than scratching away in ledgers and so was just a hoax. The vanishing countryside of my boyhood — now criss-crossed with new houses — affected me with a personal sense of loss, the more acute now that I was working all day in the city and saw no more than a patch of blue tenting over the black warehouses. It was 1921, the year of the unending heatwave.

Yet God had always been my friend. What he was, or how he came to be, or what he could accomplish, did not matter. One felt him there behind the seen world, increasing one's stature, exalting one's soul like the splendour of a summer day divined in a shuttered room. A twilight was falling over that outer day, that other sun. Peake could not see that I did not want to listen now that I knew he did not believe. He stared at my averted head.

'Not necessarily silly. And after all what do you mean by soul?' He rubbed his boot along the greasy mire at the pavement edge and rumpled his sprinkled hair with his hand. Oh not again, not again, I thought. A coldness fell between us but I was so afraid of losing him as well as God that I could not reply with the asperity that would have served with Wilson.

'What do you mean?' I asked in the small voice of misery, after a long silence.

'Well, Les,' he said, taking my arm and squeezing it, desperately trying to be friendly, to make me feel better. 'Lots of people — scientists, I mean — say only matter exists for instance.'

In Bishopsgate the gigantic stone facades of banks and offices stood up like quarry faces — they were matter. Around me crowds were surging to the stations — they were matter. There was Peake's voice — was that matter? Then mind — what about mind?

I blurted it out.

'What about mind? What about that then? What about all that goes on in your mind? You can't see it, but you believe in it!'

A shadow of annoyance passed over his face, extinguishing the friendliness. He dropped my arm.

'Mark you, don't let me influence you — but what's the point of God? What's the point? I just don't get the point.'

We were back in Bishopsgate after walking the whole length of Houndsditch and back.

'Speaking as a biologist,' he said, 'you don't need to

postulate God. The idea's a nuisance — a survival, superstition.'

Eric Peake lent me books on the theme of evolution and biology. He was not a biologist, of course, but a clerk, who dreamed of being a biologist as an escape from his futile job. Joseph McCabe was one author I remember. He had been a monk and written an *exposé* of his monastic order. Now, with the angular passion of the convert, he had become a leading polemical opponent of Christianity. More formidable was a rigorous, pedantic German, Ernst Haeckel. Two other authors were Edward Clodd and Ralph Ingersoll. I did not understand them all but had no difficulty in grasping their conclusions. I read them on the bus and going home in the train and in bed till the candle guttered out. Their importance was that they presented me with the first organized system of ideas I had come upon. Perhaps I had not grasped until that moment that the world and its life could even be conceived in such a way.

8

Before reading about evolution, I should probably have accepted unconsciously T. E. Hulme's view that the world was only organized in parts (the parts I personally knew, of course), and the rest was cinders. In effect the books said that science revealed that animate and inanimate things were subject to discoverable laws and behaved in predictable ways. New events flowed inescapably out of a succession of earlier causes. The freely-acting, freely-willing living thing was an illusion. It had no more right to consider itself free than a football kicked about a field by twenty-two players. A new word — determinism — swam like a comet of ill-omen into my ken. Everything that was happening flowed back to a first cause (if there was a first cause! — eternity could stretch backwards too!) and you could if you liked think of the first cause as God, but that was rather a pathetic thing to do, for it was a long time ago, and we knew nothing about it and there was just no evidence that God had ever intervened in the natural order once it had been set going, or even that it

45

needed God to set it going. If he had founded the order then he had abandoned it to its own laws and devices. So if there was a God it was useless to ask for his intercession in worldly affairs. In all, belief in God was unnecessary, a form of self-indulgence. The peoples of the world had worshipped lots of different Gods with contradictory characteristics. But that was because they were ignorant and a prey to uncontrolled emotions and not scientific like Joseph McCabe and Ernst Haeckel. All religions had opposed science and discovery in case they weakened the hold of the churches upon the super-stitious ordinary folk. Genesis was nonsense: the world was not created in seven days but in millions of years. Jesus Christ was possibly a myth — certainly his miracles were only fairy stories. His disciples had spread the story of his resurrection in order to give themselves power over simple superstitious peasant minds.

The real thing was evolution. Life had evolved with great difficulty from non-living matter and man had evolved from lesser living things after a struggle of incredible length in which weaker species and individuals were slaughtered. Even the very plants were at war, T. H. Huxley said. Man was the finest result of evolution, though he might be replaced by superman, because he was still evolving out of ages of super-stition into ages of science and enlightenment: religion was one of the things he was evolving *from*: *this was called progress*.

I searched every nook and cranny of this evolutionary universe with a thoroughness worthy of the astronomer Lap-lace or the first Russian astronauts and could find no God.

The theory shattered absolutely the conception, absorbed in childhood, of a homely universe in to which we are sent by a personal Creator, who watches our progress, is accessible to our prayers, and to whom we return for judgement when we die. It raised more acutely those other problems about the personal nature of God which seemed so impossible to answer. In what form did he exist? How could he really send his son down to earth to be betrayed and to die? Nor aid him by word and sign in that last agony? And miracles, what of them, particularly comic miracles like turning water into wine or blasting a fig tree? How could God be a trinity? Oh so many things accepted without thought, or never explained

46

in terms I could grasp, now had to face a fierce, intransigent, scornful inquiry.

Though I prayed, it seemed that God was silent. I could not resist the fear that he was silent because he was not there. The awful compulsion came upon me to say, 'There is no God.' Incertitude was the worst of all – it made me ill. I thought about it all day long and in consequence did my work badly and was cautioned, but was so miserable I did not care. The sack would only have been one disaster more. In moments when it would seem that I had forgotten the problem, it would intrude itself suddenly into my consciousness and my heart would give a leap of anguish, my body a physical start. For the new disbelief possessed all the marks of hateful treachery and, so complex was my state, I pitied the increased loneliness of the God I still thought of as a person, and was like Peter about to deny, like Judas to betray.

One morning during these months of indecision, I woke with so deep and strange an oppression in my breast that I fancied it was the onset of an illness. Yet my head did not ache and there was no fever in my limbs. What was it then that hung over me? What was it I had to remember?

Of course. There is no God. I tried in the limpid morning to understand this, to curl my mind round it as I smelled the bacon frying in the kitchen below and heard it sizzling in the pan and listened to the bustling noises of the house summoning me imperatively into the morning routine. How should I be able to eat my breakfast or go to work with this grief on my mind?

There is no God, I said aloud, to the ceiling, testing the sound of it and the heavens did not fall and crush me. The window looked out on the backyards of the square of dingy houses, on the broken fences, on the untidy chicken runs, on our rose arbour the wind had blown flat. A cock crowed on the shed of a neighbour's run and I waited for it to crow twice more. The old gentleman across the way with the silver hair and the trapped look was standing domestically at his back door in red carpet slippers, smoking his pipe and regarding the gentle autumn rain with timid disapproval. His wife was mad and hid herself in the coal cellar during thunderstorms. The trimmed hawthorn in Mrs Brown's yard was a dull green hummock spangled with raindrops. The

47

clothes-line was silver too. Only the ash tree was triumphant, spurting upwards, indifferent to metaphysics, a slender green fountain, a living banner, a spear. Yet all had changed, shrunk, grown meaner and somehow more despicable. I had too. God had died. There was no glory.

I rubbed my finger along the rough stone window ledge, feeling the strange nature of that unthinking stuff, and pressed my forehead against the cold glass and stared at my hand moving of its own will in an emptied world. Even that too had become a stranger.

9

Yet it was after I had decided that I no longer believed in God that a new revelation occurred and set me in tumult. Lord Devonport, who had founded Kearley and Tonge and the International Stores, and had been Food Controller during the war, lived at Great Marlow. Lady Devonport would frequently send a hurried grocery order for half a pound of china tea and a plum cake to Mitre Square and ask for immediate delivery. One Saturday she rang up for her china tea and, the only office boy willing to volunteer, I was bundled off with a small parcel and a few shillings to Great Marlow where a Rolls-Royce with a uniformed driver picked me up and bore me and my absurd cargo to a large country house. It was the first time I had ridden in a private vehicle, unless one counted the painful uncushioned pillion-seat of my cousin's motor bike. Nevertheless after tea and plumcake at the great house I refused to ride back in the car. I had seen from the whirling country lanes a vista of the Thames in springtime, with mile upon mile of rolling beechwoods and flowering hawthorns, and insisted upon walking. This was my Saturday afternoon and I wanted to enjoy it and make it last for as long as possible. I should have fought anybody who tried to put me back into the car again.

All along the lane on the crest of the downs, spring lay warm and fragrant. The valley odours and the sharp smell of water came up from the river. The beechwood was transparently green, and silver limbs curved downwards into green

48

misted caves on fire with last year's leaves. After day upon day in the noisy fringes of the East End it was intoxicating, and I sat upon a bank to let the sun soak into me, throwing my bowler hat on to the grass behind me and forgetting my train home. Across the river thunderheads massed, piling dazzling snows upon purple in the sunshine. The world slipped gradually away and I felt only the burning sun and the serenity, and looked down upon the green torrent of the beeches flowing to the river and longed to glissade down them into the indigo water. Not a house could be seen, nor a man, and the silence was intense. I was full of gratitude for my absolute solitude.

The sun clouded while I was resting there and I heard unexpectedly the roar of a waterfall, and looking up saw the rain rushing down the vale in one opaque wall of the silver and silk of its own smoke, blotting out the beechwoods. A herd of cows lifted startled heads in the field below me, and, some racial memory stirring them, turned suddenly and raced from the lances of the rain across ancestral prairies. I picked up my bowler to run and found shelter only under some pines growing above a lichened wall by the roadside, and squeezed myself anxiously under them as the cloudburst reached me.

To shelter was futile. The warm rain deluged me. The gutter of my bowler filled up and a shower-bath looped and cascaded from its rim. My shabby clothes soaked it up and my cheap and wretched collar became pulp. 'Why hide from the rain?' I asked myself. It has been drenching things from time immemorial and there was no reason to be afraid of it. I accepted madness and doffed my useless bowler and lifted my face. The torrents drenched my hair and ran in streams down my neck. The taste of the rain was pure, and its smell exhilarated me.

The storm went as quickly as it came, and the sun shining fiercely through the purified air upon the steaming woods caused the whole golden scented atmosphere to boil. Even through my wet clothes the sun burnt me. After the roar of water, the earth crouched in silence and stillness, then as though at an unseen conductor's beat, simultaneously across the valley every hushed unseen bird broke into song. The cleared sky was as blue as a kingfisher's wing. A gust of rapture swept powerfully through me, and for what then occurred within there are no words. When you are gazing at the flat mirrored surface of a river, perfect in its own dimension, unflawed by depth, a moment will come, if you continue to watch, when you are suddenly aware that the perfect surface has gone and cannot be restored and that what indeed you see are the depths of the river, with their complex, shifting bronze lights and misted brown landscape and sinuous shadows where fish glide silent and alive. It is a moment that cannot be willed, that comes slowly as the eyes focus, and always with the same shock of recognition.

In the same way, and with the same shock, I stared through the celestial landscape. It was not itself, it was merely the intimation of a majesty beyond it. It was the translucent surface through which an unbearable glory shone. I was unable to move, so profound was the sensation of the unreality of what lay just beyond me. A few months before, I should have thought of God and prayed, for the intimation of a presence was irresistible, but I no longer believed in him and it was therefore impossible that I should have visions of him. But if I could not think in terms of a personal God there was nothing to deny pantheism to me. It was quite possible to believe in Eric Peake's universe yet to think of it as divine (I argued with myself). Indeed a quotation attributed to Pythagoras, 'As if Divinity dwelt not in the very atoms,' had been haunting me for days. It seemed to resolve at once that love of God which I was able to discard only with the greatest difficulty, with love of nature, my consoler, and all the theories of evolution and materialism my head was aching with the effort to absorb and justify.

Not easily to forget, I tore down branches of pine from the trees around me and carried them back through trains and tubes and trams, to deck the walls of the spare bedroom which I had taken over as a study. The smell of the pinewoods would always be about the house. One day, many years later, during my Army service, I was given a little wooden cell among the pinewoods of Mount Carmel to live in. It had no windows, only wire screens through which drifted day and night the pine incense. I lay awake struggling to recall what it roused in me with such poignancy that it was like a pain, like Marcel Proust with his madeleine. Quite suddenly I saw the odd poetic boy I had been, in his handed-down green tweed suit, and rain-warped bowler, sitting alone in a railway carriage, the richly scented pine boughs clutched to him, the hot spring day filtering through them to his thirsty young heart. H. G. Wells would have warmed to him.

10

I discovered Richard Jefferies' *The Story of My Heart* in my teens in the year that H. M. Tomlinson told Henry Williamson that it was 'a most dangerous book'. There has been more than one cult of Jefferies; the first led by H. S. Salt in the eighties, the last a very fine rescue of early manuscripts and drafts for which Samual Looker was responsible at the time of the centenary after the Second World War. Jefferies is one of the greatest nature writers England ever threw up on the periphery of the romantic movement, but an observer, even a poet-observer, a countryman, not a meticulous field natural-ist. I do not know that he ever collected specimens for a cabinet. It was not easy to rhapsodize about specimens pinned under glass. Perhaps indeed we have Wordsworth to thank for the cult of landscape, flower and folklore to which Jefferies and W. H. Hudson witnessed.

What will live of Jefferies, apart from *The Story of My Heart*, could well be those wonderfully accurate accounts of the country men and women into which historians will one day dip. What historians of religion, I wonder, know 'The Country Sunday', so vivid and trenchant, or that great novel of a decaying farming family *Amaryllis at the Fair* which Jefferies dictated to his wife as he lay dying at his house at Goring in Sussex! Henry Williamson did a service to literature and history by reviving and editing the 1880 *Hodge and His Masters*. But in some of his writing Jefferies achieved a burn-ing, passionate identification with his subject, of the kind Traherne mastered, and a style, at once incantatory and intense, which sweeps the reader before him. Most of all is this true of his Nietzschean essay, *The Story of My Heart*. He is on fire there to wrest from himself and from nature a sense of transcendence over the accidents of life. He cannot bear

51

the crumbling of all things, or his own inability to move through time and to realize everything that had come to pass on the Wiltshire downs he chose for his meditations. He seeks to enter into the very being, in *The Story of My Heart*, of what touches, moves him upon his chosen hilltops: grass, earth, cloud, sun, the tumuli of dead kings, the whitened skulls of foxes. His own resort is prayer, ceaseless wordless prayer by which his soul-life grows and he plunges and merges his being into everything that is. He was, appropriate to his age, superman praying to 'superdeo' — which was his word for the transcendent. Whatever else one says of him — that he was a little dotty, and very poor, and unhappy in his Victorian world and in the end so desperately ill that all he could see was the tent of sky through his sickroom window — what counts most about him still is that he was so spiritually alive. *The Story of My Heart* is the fierce recapture by a dying man of what he lived by. Perhaps one needs to point, after him, not to any would-be pagan writer of the same genre, but to two Jesuits, the poet Gerard Manley Hopkins, who like Jefferies was awed by the holiness of natural things and as full of grief and care as he was, and Teilhard de Chardin, for whom, one suspects, in the end, the majestic onward sweep of the universe was God enough.

For me, in my teens, *The Story of My Heart* was almost too moving to bear. It was the discovery of a new poet. The purity and simplicity of the language exalted me: its rhythm ran daily through my head. It spoke to my condition in a way that transfixed me. Here was no adolescent but a man, a poet and a naturalist as I sought then to be, whose experiences were my experiences and voices my voices too, who knew the city, and was sometimes desolate in it, and stood overwhelmed by the crowds at Mansion House, and who had done as I, untutored and alone, had done — sought solitary places, prayed with his face to the grass or ear to the wind under sun and stars, forcing himself to enter into the being of the turning world. It was frightening to be so well understood and it was at the same time, in his words, soul enlarging: I could not feel so odd or eccentric after that in my spiritual exercises in those set places of pilgrimage I had chosen. By uncanny chance one walk of mine took me past the German church and across the railway line at Forest Hill to Sydenham

Park where grew some great sombre cedars which deeply impressed me. Indeed I walked that way often just to look at them. I had no idea that Jefferies' aunt and uncle once lived there, in Shanklin Villa, and that he as a youth often stayed there, as impressed with the cedars as I had been. Nor did I know that when he wrote *The Story of My Heart* he was a man dying from tuberculosis of the intestines, and a fistula, and that what is still a young man's book (he finished it when he was thirty-five) was a passionate protest from one who lived for the sun at the closing in of darkness and death.

> Do not go gentle into that good night.
> Rage, rage against the dying of the light.

He was that rage.

> The great sun burning with Light, (Jefferies wrote) the strong earth, dear earth; the warm sky; the pure air; the thought of ocean; the inexpressible beauty of all filled me with a rapture, an ecstasy, an inflatus. With this inflatus too, I prayed. Next to myself I came and recalled myself, my bodily existence. I held out my hand, the sunlight gleamed on the skin and the iridescent nails; I recalled the mystery and beauty of the flesh. I thought of the mind with which I could see the ocean sixty miles distant, and gather to myself its glory. I thought of my inner existence, that consciousness which is called the soul. These, that is, myself - I threw into the balance to weigh the prayer the heavier. My strength of body, mind and soul, I flung into it; I put forth my strength: I wrestled and laboured, and toiled in might of prayer. The prayer, this soul-emotion was in itself — not for an object — it was a passion. I hid my face in the grass, I was wholly prostrated, I lost myself in the wrestle. I was rapt and carried away.

Those mewling philistines who shrank in Jefferies' day and since from the passionate self-revelation of those passages were unaware of the nature of great mystical writing, which was out of tune with utilitarianism and evangelicalism, for both of which a muscular Christianity was more appropriate. Traherne could write in just such an abandonment (and for hundreds of pages):

Send down the Holy Ghost upon me: Breathe upon me, inspire me, quicken me, illuminate me, enflame me, fill me with the Spirit of God; that I may overflow with praises and thanksgivings as they (the apostles) did. Fill me with the riches of Thy glory, that Christ may dwell in my heart by faith, that I being rooted and grounded in Love may speak the wonderful work of God. Let me be alive unto them: let me see them all, let me feel them all, let me enjoy them all: that I may admire the greatness of Thy love unto my soul, and rejoice in communion with Thee for evermore. How happy, O Lord, am I. . . .[2]

And then there was, if further proof one needs, St John of the Cross — 'Verses written after an ecstasy of high exaltation':

> So borne aloft, so drunk-reeling,
> So rapt was I, so swept away,
> Within the scope of sense or feeling
> My sense or feeling could not stay.
> And in my soul I felt, revealing,
> A sense that, though its sense was naught,
> Transcended knowledge with my thought.[3]

Transcending knowledge with his thought. Yes, that was what Jefferies was doing in an abandonment truly in the western mystical tradition which perhaps the apostles set in motion at Pentecost when they were accused of being drunk. If Jefferies had planted himself in the Christian tradition there would now be little pious books about him carried around by the Children of Mary and perhaps little medallions to wear. But he was hostile, and so Christian thought steered delicately around him. But how could the humanists of the age of Bentham, Mill, Marx and Darwin bear the man who hymned the universe with his face in the buttercups on a hill-top? They were all as buttoned up as their frock coats.

I had no hesitations before his raptures. They spoke to my condition. I shared his divine rage for life and holiness. Yet I was not ready to follow him everywhere. I could half-apprehend his view of the meaningless of time to the soul.

[2] *Centuries of Meditation* (Dobell 1934), p. 70.
[3] *Poems of St John of the Cross*, tr. Roy Campbell (Harvill 1951), p. 31.

It is eternity now. I am in the midst of it. It is about me in the sunshine; I am in it, as the butterfly floats in the light-laden air. Nothing has to come; it is now. Now is eternity; now is the immortal life. Here this moment, by this tumulus, on earth, now; I exist in it.

And there was his intuition that man's presence in the universe brought all to life and light. Without his consciousness burning away within it the universe would be a dead thing, Jefferies taught, and this struck my understanding. But I, just then accepting evolution, and therefore pattern and meaning in the cosmos, could not bear:

All nature, as far as we can see, is anti- or ultra-human, outside, and has no concern with men. . . . Centuries of thought have failed to reconcile and fit the mind to the universe, which is designless, and purposeless, and without idea.

I sprang angrily back from that. But how prophetic he was! One great scientific problem of our day is whether the universe is hostile or benevolent or simply indifferent to men. Hostile, not in some motivated sense, but in the poverty of conditions which promote and sustain life. Man clings to such a thin skin of life-savings conditions, his biosphere, on a tiny space ship in a barren atmosphere while the universe goes on with the business of making and breaking galaxies. But I kicked at all that kind of talk then. Everything *had* to make sense. I think most of the contemporaries of Jefferies, spell-bound by science, would have agreed with me.

11

Yet I see how, with Jefferies, the invisible worm of self-consciousness first burrowed in and the rose became sick. What had been almost inarticulate in my life became literary overnight. Jefferies was so overpowering. How would Jefferies describe this experience? I would ask myself, no doubt meaning how would I describe it if I could write as well as he? My solitary worship became something I could cultivate, develop, exaggerate if I chose to. I chose not to. My passion had been so private and I so self-effacing that I would never have dreamed of describing it even to my closest friend. Description would have *destroyed* it. It entered a little into the ethos of my first prose writings, because in those things I tended to rhapsodize about nature, but it was absent from the even more awful poems I wrote then, which seem mostly to have been about love, and were burnt.

The gales of scepticism blew me towards empiricism anyway. I was more ready to ask myself what those soul experiences really meant, really added up to, because there was some jeering suburban noise in the back of my head ready to convict me of a literary pose. So though Jefferies widened my understanding of myself, and enchanted me, and my whole life would be poorer without him, he inevitably, in the end, by setting such experiences outside me and making them objective, enabled me to criticize them. It would be wrong to say that I now rejected my nature-mysticism. That I could not do, for it could still sweep through me unawares and I have never lost the sense, which one finds above all in the impressionist painters, of a physical world penetrated by another light. Simply, I turned from it, doggedly, obstinately. Meaning was not to be found there and meanings, explanations, were necessary. There was no mainspring of social action in what might be no more than a psychological self-indulgence.

It was not so difficult then as it might seem to shut the door of my mind on this other dimension. Young manhood is too full sometimes to bear: it has more experiences than can be handled. There were occasional pangs of inward poverty or the dry rising of a forgotten desolation when I read that Charles Darwin lost all delight in poetry and music in his later years and blamed this decay of the spirit on too scientific and cerebral a life: or when I read (in his *Autobiography*) that John Stuart Mill had asked himself whether joy and happiness would be his if all the Benthamite reforms he believed in were at that moment realized, and vigorously answered 'No' to himself. He saw that if a life were to be lived only at his master Jeremy's level, then it was not worth the living.

If you no longer go to the well to drink, why complain if it cannot refresh you? Still, there was more than a simple choice involved. The neglected friend is not only forgotten but forgets. In an essay on 'The Love of God and Affliction', Simone Weil speaks of how an infinity of time and space separate us, who are at the point of distance where God can hardly reach us, from the love of God. We cannot cross this desert, but God, she says, crosses this infinity of time and space and comes to us. He comes in his own time and we have only the power to consent to his nuptial visit or to reject him. 'If we are deaf, he comes back again and again like a beggar, but also, like a beggar one day he stops coming.'

PART TWO

Everyone suddenly burst out singing
SIEGFRIED SASSOON

1

When I left Kearley and Tonge in the East End because they
would not increase my wage by two shillings and sixpence a
week — I was earning a pound — I went to work for my
father, in Fleet Street, for thirty shillings: barely a survival
wage. I tried to supplement it by writing and had some pieces
accepted by *The Open Road*, a monthly magazine intended
to attract the readers of *The Trail*, a London scout magazine
which had closed down, and to cater for the new hiking
craze. I was able to help the monthly by calling on advertising
agents in Fleet Street and suddenly found myself invited to
manage it at the princely sum, to me, of four pounds a week.
Of course I accepted. I found myself, lately an office boy,
with an office and an office boy, called Jenkinson, of my
own and my name in black paint on the frosted glass of the
door, in Denison House at Victoria, by what was then the
tram terminus. The building and my old office are still there.
The change was dazzling. I thought myself made for life. I
was not yet eighteen. The best was yet to come! The Editor
resigned and I was made Editor-Manager. And that was put on
the door too. It was natural that I should want all my friends
to see this and I would have little parties in my office in the
evening. We would sit round the office fire (coal, ninepence a
scuttle) and talk and drink tea. I never got to the office before
ten and I divided the lunch hours between prowling round
the Tate and National Galleries and sculling on the Serpen-
tine. I found after a while that I was writing most of the
paper myself. I bought myself a Harris tweed suit and match-
ing tweed hat, and prospected a bungalow at Caterham, preparing to become a poet-editor-country gentleman in the already defunct Georgian style, and even, with the nature-writer
Marcus Woodward, hunted down in the Chilterns near Princes
Risborough the Pink and Lily pub where Rupert Brooke had
written a contribution to the visitors' book which began:

> Never came there to the Pink
> Two such men as we I think!
> Never came there to the Lily
> Two men quite so richly silly . . .

I sold the story of that entry to *The Daily Herald* for a guinea. I cannot now remember who Brooke's partner was. Perhaps it was Edward Marsh, Brooke's friend and patron. I met him at the Royal Society of Literature many years later and was awed, so old was he, that this was even possible: meeting Masefield there too had the same effect on me.

I had no patron and only a few pounds saved when *The Open Road* went bankrupt. We tried to sell the lively little monthly to one of the Fleet Street combines, but none would have it. I had to appear at Carey Street. I bought some of the office furniture at a knockdown price and set myself up in an otherwise barren suburban room as a freelance journalist. That lasted six months, then my savings ran out, and I was back in Fleet Street, with my father, earning my thirty shillings a week, and no one else anxious to take on so young an editor of a newly busted paper.

If I took these setbacks lightly it was because I was totally absorbed in youth movements and my nascent socialism. I canvassed that autumn for the return of Percy Alden for the Tottenham constituency as a paid worker: I think pay and travel expenses came to about three pounds a week. One just managed. When that was over, and Percy Alden had lost, I went back to the unfurnished suburban room which cost me a few shillings a week and, tiring of sending out articles and poems no one wanted, wrote a book. All trace of the book has long since vanished. I cannot remember what it was about or even its title. I recall only an effort to talk about the beech-woods of the Chilterns in the autumn and to describe the bodgers at work on their primitive lathes. I suspect the book was an effort to combine Richard Jefferies' nature essays as in *Life in a Southern County*, which I had picked up for six-pence in a shop in Steyning, with Edward Carpenter's uplifting *Towards Democracy*, which a friend had pushed at me. A heady mixture. But then it was something, at that age, I suppose, to have the stamina to write a full-length affair, however bad. None of the manuscripts of those years have survived, not even the bound copies of *The Open Road* which a faithless friend borrowed from me and never returned. I wrote a play called *The Devil Brews Punch*, based on the Hindhead Murders, for the producer of *Sweeney Todd*. I knew him through my father. He looked at the list of characters on the title page, grunted that there were too many, said he would read it, put it in his bag and I never saw it again. I became hardened to these defeats.

I was sixteen or so when I came out of Scouting and joined John Hargrave's new movement, Kibbo Kift (or 'proof of great strength'), overwhelmed by its colour, its romance, its boldness, its Red Indian lore. Osbert Walter and I had already devoured Ernest Thompson Seton's *The Book of Woodcraft and Indian Lore*, and we had read Hargrave's articles in *The Scout* and were ready to worship at strange shrines.

At the end of the First World War Hargrave broke with the Scouts and founded his own movement, the queerly titled Kibbo Kift Kindred, whose members wandered around with gray and green jerkins and cowls and decorated rucksacks. At the invitation of Eric Peake, Osbert Walter and I became members.

What Hargrave was seeking to do he set out in a giant manifesto, *The Great War Brings It Home*, a book of nearly four hundred pages, illustrated by the author, published in 1919, but begun by him before the war, when he was only seventeen: the title points out that the war itself underlined his case for national reconstruction and social regeneration. He wanted a new life-style based on the lessons of the savage races, and educational and social systems which turned back towards the primitive. But his great unreadable book, which only social historians will ever quarry now, is lavish with advice on everything — venereal disease, sex, camping techniques, tribal life, crafts, nature and the unnatural, transcendental meditation and religion of a pantheistic sort. It shocked his Boy Scout admirers for its indifference to formal Christianity.

Unintentionally I became a leader among the South London groups, which were mostly left wing. I was in this way drawn into the Labour Party. The Kibbo Kift groups who elected me met in the Council Chamber of the beautiful old Deptford Town Hall in 1922. John Wilmot — subsequently Lord Wilmot — was in the chair. I was shocked by my election and could only stutter when asked to make a speech. 'Get on with it man,' said Wilmot in irritation. On with what? That nonplussed me. But in the year or so that I was editing *The Open Road*, I was already, unwillingly, having a row with Hargrave

63

because he said I was too young to hold office in the Kibbo Kift. It was a stupid affair because, at its height, I was no more than six months from my eighteenth birthday, the qualifying age for adult membership. Nevertheless he refused to recognize me in my office, or the local association itself, perhaps simply because he wanted to get rid of left wingers and other troublesome people.

Yet here I was editing a paper intended to appeal to *all* open-air and camping people! I went as editor to see Baden-Powell, then a pink ageing baby, to seek some reconciliation with the Scouts for the sake of circulation, and I made an arrangement to spend a weekend with Hargrave, both to help *The Open Road* and to end the absurd quarrel over my age.

My sensible proposal to parley privately with Hargrave produced a passionate storm in the North London group of which I was also a member and which often gathered at my *Open Road* offices in Denison House. We were an ambitious lodge. Our noteheading tells why. We limited the number of our members to the mystic seven, each one specializing in a branch of learning.

THE

ANKH ☥ LODGE

A

CHAPTER

of

Seven Erudites

Endeavouring to Promote

UNITY

Upon Earth

℥℥

The Ankh Lodge had its own quarrel with Hargrave, because of the tumultuous and aggressive character of our strange leader, Eric Peake, whose enormous skull seemed to have derived directly from Neanderthal Man. Peake, despite his official atheism, believed in the occult. He also felt rejected by Hargrave, even persecuted, and wrote long diatribes to me about this. I believe his membership had just been suspended. He was under the impression that John Hargrave was using black magic and various demonic and occult practices against *him* personally. Indeed, he was obsessed with this and various other fears of rejection by Hargrave, and had long engaged in a stupefying correspondence with him, of accusation and counter-accusation of which I knew only the vaguest details. My sensible proposal to visit Hargrave on my own seemed to Peake like a 'betrayal'. I had gone over to the enemy. He said this and similar bitter things, as though Hargrave were not our leader, but a deadly foe. If I went to see Hargrave privately I would be thrown out. I weakly gave in and cancelled my visit. I could not bear to lose all my friends at once: though mad, they were precious.

In the end, Kibbo Kift broke up. My South London groups and others seceded at a great meeting at High Wycombe in 1924. Hargrave went on with what was left to found a Social Credit Party whose disciplined greenshirts marched like fascists. I lost touch with Eric Peake and Osbert Walter. In 1925, I and a friend, Sidney Shaw, founded a new movement, the Woodcraft Folk, in a South London suburb. We could not bear that all this picturesque and significant life-style should collapse and come to nothing. We gathered four or five boys together in Rushey Green and began camping, and in the autumn added a group of girls. The movement still thrives with myself as its Old Man, and in 1975 celebrated its jubilee.

Soon I was busy writing books and plays, poems and songs for it. (It is one of the oddities of my life that I was taught Indian dancing by Ernest Thompson Seton in a dusty gaslit chapel in the Whitechapel Road.) In an idealistic charter our new movement pledged itself to develop 'mental and physical health' for 'the service of the people'. We undertook 'to camp out and live in close contact with nature and to use the creative faculties both of our minds and our hands'. We pledged ourselves 'to make ourselves familiar with the history of the world and the development of man in the slow march of evolution that we may understand and revere the Great Spirit which urges all things to perfect themselves'. We concluded by asserting that the 'instruments of production' should be owned by the community and all necessities 'produced by common service for the common use'. And in the first pamphlet, *The Child and the Race* (1926), I wrote, 'We are the revolution. With the health that is ours and with the intellect and physique that will be the heritage of those we train we are paving the way for that reorganization of the economic system which will mark the rebirth of the human race'.

However, the quite strong ideological justifications of our movement, so evident in its training programmes such as *The Child and the Race* and *The Training of Pioneers* (1936), hardly matter here where I am speaking of its spiritual impact. They were perhaps not of first importance even then, in 1925. We could have held all those socialist ideas without our particular life-style. The truth was that we were bonded together by our camp fellowship.

Every activity in town was nothing more than a dusty substitute for life in the open. We were a brotherhood of the campfire, for the fire, in the council circle, was the heart of every camp. The first years are haunted by those glowing, roasting 'council fires' which we lit in the early evening. Round the fire we sang songs and told stories, ate a supper of cocoa, biscuits and cheese, and so reluctant were the young leaders to depart to their tents that the movement was often (justly) criticized for keeping children up too late on these many festive occasions. We sang songs, told stories, and the older folk argued politics and religion far into the night. Tardily arriving we strode down the hill towards the thrilling storm of singing voices. We had heard this compelling note far away: it had excited us to hurry when the fire in the distance was no more than a single coal burning in the mist. Now to see, as one came near, the disembodied faces of one's friends and girls in that rosy gleam was to come longingly home to the fellowship one loved with all one's heart.

No camp was complete without a campfire. Beside it, when the night grew late, the young self-conscious herald stood up. Last night he was a schoolboy in baggy grey flannels and worn blue blazer, a cap holding down his shock of chestnut hair. Tonight his hair fell over his brow, a bronze mane the firelight made molten. Tonight he wore a silk surcoat of blue and gold, surmounted by a crowing cock in scarlet. He stepped into the circle and said, with uplifted hand:

Now doth the blackness of night encircle us
And the night wind whispers in the larches:
Now doth night enfold us like a cloak
And the earth is still, save for the owls and the beasts
    that hunt,
And we, the Woodcraft Folk, have assembled in festivity
Since the setting of the sun,
Now the flames flicker and die,
And the ashes grow grey upon the folkstead.

To which the leader replied:
To your tents, O woodcrafters
and may stillness ride over the camp.
May you sleep and rise refreshed
When the light sparkles on the dew wet grass.
Peace!
Peace be to all men. Peace.

Then we sang 'The Campfire Carol.'
Presently the circle would break and the boys and girls, blanket laden, rustle through the wet grass to their tents, set in a circle round the campfire, which presently the candles and torches transformed into a string of blowing Chinese lanterns.

In the morning the herald would reappear and standing by the dead campfire would shout:

All ye who dwell within the camp
Awake! Arise!
For the earth has cast off the black cap of night
And is arrayed in the white garment of day
All ye who dwell within the camp
Awake! Arise!

And there is the heart of the thing — the living of a kind of poetry, which so answered the emotional hungers of the young people who joined that they joined for life. Perhaps it is significant that the first class I ever ran for leaders — in the East Lewisham Labour Party H.Q. in Brownhill Road,

Catford — was on 'The Lakeland Poets'.

In one of the poems I wrote for the Wayfarers, the pioneer group which I founded, I tried to express what the magic meant for little city boys and girls:

> Through the woods in Indian File
> Hushed and drowsed with sun the while
> Dim green shadows arch and fall
> Round us, a mysterious wall
> Of woven boughs and breaks of sun
> Caught by the leaves they dance upon:
>
> Through the woods in Indian style
> A softly, eager-prowling file,
> Wondering what the leaves hold there
> Captive in the shadowy air
> What strange things may swiftly rise
> To set us trembling in surprise.
>
> Then somewhere by leaf shadows hid
> A valiant blackbird winds unbid
> His elfin horn, and this domain
> Seems more silent for the strain.
> So it is true what old folk say,
> A piper comes this way to play.

There were other poems, less A. A. Milne-ish. This 'Invocation', which *The Observer* published in 1928, for instance:

> Francis, by your dryad oath,
> Francis, by the virgin wild,
> From towns and from the Midas touch,
> From losing all and gaining much
> Keep my brothers undefiled.
> Apollo of the seeing eye
> And Pan by your sweet wantonness
> Save me from life in deathliness
> From bookish eyes that see no sun,
> And watch no stars their aeons run,
> From lips which are untouched with dew,
> From craftless hand and failing thew,
> From wheezy breath and waxen ears
> And mind forgetting sunny years,
> From all that makes a man a slave,

68

From living one foot in the grave,
Apollo, Pan and Francis — *save*!

I had celebrated my worship of evolution, which clearly
I had tried to impose on my new movement, with a long,
atrocious poem, 'The Song of Creation', which nevertheless
had a certain vogue among the first members. It was an untutored Whitmanesque litany which rejoiced in the passage
of the *élan vital* from the primordial past down to us, at the
moment of the birth of our movement in the twenties, and
proclaimed

> ... out of the ashes of the old shall arise the new resplen-
> dent city and the resurrected race,
> And the starved of body, the starved of mind and the
> starved of light shall be no more.

Yet there were other passages which spoke with realism
about the sick post-1918 world and reveal something of the
genesis of the movement and more about me. I should not
now shrink from this adolescent effort had it all been at this
level.

> The people pass and repass in the street,
> Torn posters flap from garish hoardings,
> The trams rattle along, and messenger boys with perky
> faces whistle music-hall ditties,
> Mothers hurry past with bowed heads and weary eyes to
> do their shopping,
> The unemployed shuffle along or lean against the walls and
> gaze into nothingness,
> And I am frightened and made ill by their dazed and
> despairing faces.
> Under a black human tide the red flags swarm out of Poplar
> And thunder through the city.
>
> A train rumbles over a bridge and its smoke wreathes down
> into the dusty street,
> Cranes and derricks swing from factory walls and the work-
> men shout and sweat as they unload their drays,
> The backing horses sweat and exert their knotted muscles
> and there is fear in their eyes and dilated nostrils,
> But the carter only curses their stumbling and clattering
> (But even here, can I, the Song, be heard).

Washing flaps in dingy backyards and dirty children gambol
in the gutters,
From the mouths of babes and sucklings issues forth the
accumulated lingual filth of civilization,
I peer into drab houses, with their rickety stairs and faded
wallpaper,
I peer into crowded rooms where men and women herd
together, and grumble and grouse about work and one
another,
And go out and buy an evening edition for the racing, I
peer into the huddled minds of little children and divine
their fears and their agonies, and their minds steeped in
the futility of the grown-up,
(I peer and am sorry)

I peer into backyards where the closet door swings open
on broken hinges and the dustbin overflows with garbage
and stench.
And lo! a rage fills me and I would cry destruction on the
city and its evil ways,
Damning the teeming life within it to the abyss of the
forgotten,
Fear and hatred scorch my soul and I recoil and lust to
break the bonds that bind me:
For over beyond the smoke stack rises a vision of cloud
shadows on the downs, and the sun on the golden wheat,
And I would shout and rage lest the town overpower me.

Then the hatred passes and I would weep for shattered lives
and empty days.
For the agony that created nothing but this,
And my song rises clear and goes whispering into the hearts
of the crushed,
And wistful glances are cast at the sky.

All that eager life and political protest of the Folk is half a
century away now. What we are recalling seems a young and,
if not innocent, then unsophisticated world. But one has to
remember the shadow of the appalling Great War, which was
our background. Most of the new leaders were about twenty
or younger. They had not fought in the war but they had
suffered from it, and with ardour they were giving themselves

to the building of a new world. None then knew the shape it would take. A declaration used by the Wayfarers, the first group, and still thriving, expresses that youthful dedication. It derived from William Morris.

This shall be for a bond between us: that we are of one blood, you and I: that we have cried peace to all men and claimed kinship with every living thing: that we hate war and sloth and greed and love fellowship and that we shall go singing to the fashioning of a new world.

I gave something like fifteen zealous, hardworking, happy years to the movement. It was like a wife to me, and occasionally like a nagging mother-in-law or jealous mistress Soon I was a beardless patriarch to all those thousands of lively boys and girls. I was determined to live out in life all that most deeply moved me inwardly, and like a true charismatic to persuade and compel as many others as I could to go along with me. In that I certainly succeeded. What need had I of any other religion just then? Some chaps have all the luck, and when I come to visit again those green-clad boys and girls in their camps, my heart beat quickens just as it did in the twenties and thirties.

2

The euphoria that the poetic view of evolution had aroused in me so long before Teilhard received a sudden check. Some friends and I were walking the hills around my home, studying the great plain of winter stars, and talking about the cosmic as well as the human future. I was full of exaltation at the grandeur of the spinning universe but it was G. S. M. Ellis, a Cambridge botanist, who pointed out that our planet had only a limited life and would one day end up in interstellar cold. The possibility that all that planetary life and energy, all the vision and suffering I had tried to celebrate in 'The Song of Creation', led only to a frozen planet was a revelation I could not then take. If it were true, everything seemed worthless. Everyone remarked on how my spirits suddenly fell. Indeed, the check was so great I could hardly speak, after such an emotional involvement with evolution as 'the life eternal' a few moments before.

It was a salutary check. I began slowly to see that evolution involved another dimension of existence, apart altogether from the time-scale of human history. To that history, evolution provided only an inhuman, indifferent background. All those aeons past, and perhaps to come, in which there was no man present, no life even, seemed beyond comprehension. Nothing surely came out of *them* to man who had at this moment to decide whether to fight his wars or not, to live or die for his causes, or how to get a job or where to find a little love. The stars did not help, they were cold comfort. Indeed out there the galaxies pursued their cosmic dance perhaps with no witnesses save us. Indeed no witnesses could live near their inner fires or in their outer cold. All this did not kill my interest in evolution, but it did away with any passion. One could contemplate it, one could no longer worship it. I had to pull my sights down to the human and historical and cease making evolution a substitute for the God I had abandoned.

3

My mind pulls up out of the past, ten or more years after the descent of God on Marlow woods, an incident, fleeting but significant, at Wapping Old Stairs, that ancient watergate on the Thames, dark and incorrigible in its slumdom in the shiftless thirties. I was a young left-wing writer and lecturer with two novels and a book on Russia behind me; I was conceited enough to think that I had a future in politics — I had just been offered my home constituency — and I was on my way on foot through the drizzling dusk to speak at a rally organized by my own youth movement, the Woodcraft Folk.

My movement, child of my adolescence, was deeply saturated with the nature mysticism I have described and in revolt against the physical and spiritual destructiveness, as we thought it, of living in towns. We made the grassy banks on which we camped, the trees, the clouds, into gods of a sort, but we were resolutely anti-Christian. It was not surprising, of course, for we were offering a religion of a kind our-selves. The dying man on a tree made no appeal to us. He offended. And the churches! They seemed at once to be the establishment we hated and to parody it hilariously.

Yet to all that I was as an intellectual of the left in those days, had to be added a new dimension of feeling about the world which I had just then discovered with delight in Thomas Traherne. I was looting his *Centuries* with the sense of dis-covery Walt Whitman and Richard Jefferies had aroused. Like them, he confused my Marxism, though I assured myself that it was his literary genius alone which enthralled me.

I was writing the first draft of *The Living Hedge*, and in the process I had rediscovered, not with the shame that usually attends the recollection of childish gaucheness, but with affec-tion, the religious boy that I had been. The depth and sin-cerity of that boyish passion astonished me in the rationalism I now professed. I found that Traherne spoke to my boy-hood as no other writer had done, not even Jefferies, for the glory of God was constantly revealed to the infant Thomas through the natural man, and through natural things pene-trated by an eternal light. For me too, as a boy, 'the corn was orient and immortal wheat, which never should be reaped, nor was ever sown', and the dust and stones precious as gold and 'maids strange seraphic pieces of life and beauty! Boys and girls tumbling in the street, and playing, were moving jewels.' Like Thomas too I remembered that it was 'with much ado I was corrupted, and made to learn the dirty devices of this world'. Traherne electrified me with the sense of the possibility of the renewal or permanence even of the vision of Marlow woods which I had thought dead.

I can taste the atmosphere of Wapping still, but barely describe it — the lamps in zig-zag pattern diminishing down the narrow streets; the cliffs of warehouses and half-heartedly lit tenements; the unemployed still haunting the public lib-rary or lounging by the street corner pubs and shining both the walls and their jackets; the tracks of emptiness with a greasy flicker on the asphalt, and the feeling of the raw Thames tide in the November air. Not Traherne country, nor a place to be in of choice, but into that dusk an infant Thomas came hurrying, a small boy on his way to choir practice, half-skipping, half-dancing, lost in his peculiar dream, only half-seen, and singing the carol 'See amid the winter's snow' in a childish treble too fierce for the purist and with delight rousing the echoes among the tenements, giving all that he could to it. If he could, he would have thundered *Gloria in excelsis Deo* in Wapping. *Gloria in profundis Deo* in Wapping. Had I been with a companion, though, I would have commented on this innocent treble with the cynicism the times demanded, times of Hitler's rise and Russian purges, afraid to admit I was moved by it: alone, I was capable only of standing still the better to listen to the receding voice from that flitting shadow, listening with the shivering down the spine which comes in moments when a lost dimension of experience opens up again. The young voice, thrilling with its own power in the darkness, was startling enough: as astonishing just then was the breathtaking sweep of the carol itself. It had neither timidity nor apology, *only joy*. It did not fit the notion into which I (of all people) somehow talked myself over the years that religious experience was spurious and hypocritical. I was facing something, of which the child's voice was only the vehicle, I could not talk down. The faith which produced such adoration could not be entirely vacuous and fraudulent. Not then, but later, I was struck by the fact that a child's voice had spoken to my condition as accidentally as once it spoke to St Augustine's dilemma, and through music, which was the most profound and troubling of all explorations of the spirit at that point in my life.

I was troubled, too, about the meaning of the word '*spirit*', Even Christopher Caudwell, stern materialist that he was, who had great influence on us just then, talked about saving the *spiritual* activities of man. But what was spirit? Was it simply a word we gave to the kind of atmosphere generated by certain human activities, like the word 'excitement', or had it a meaning in its own right as a substantive rather than an adjectival presence in the universe, standing as surely for some reality as *matter* stood for some reality? Were they even in apposition?

William Temple, for whom I had conceived an admiration when I met him at a Workers' Educational Association function in the twenties, and whose praises Gordon Ellis had sung to me, had foxed all the trails by declaring, in *Nature, Man*

74

and God[1], that Christianity 'is the most avowedly materialist of all the great religions'. It sounded exciting at the time and gets taken up every now and then by someone who feels that something is saved for Christianity by the declaration. Nothing is. Temple was simply saying that the universe was God's universe and that nothing in it could be alien from God or man, and so a 'war' between 'spirit' and 'matter' could not truly form a part of the Christian *weltanschauung* as it was then thought to be part of the Buddhist or Hindu ethos. Indeed he talked in that book of the closeness of Christianity to the Dialectical Materialism of the Marxists which admits, if nothing else, of rational and purposive, even redemptive, impulses moving in history and in the mind of man (and surely in evolution too?). 'But a close examination of this Dialectical Materialism, strongly distinguished by its upholders from Mechanistic Materialism, suggests that its own dialectic will destroy its character as materialist, except in so far as it is opposed to the idealistic view of matter as existing only "for mind".'[2]

Temple was a dualist and believed in separate entities, mind and matter, but in a dialectical unity between them, with matter as sacramental and mind as predominant. He saw evolution as leading to the triumph of mind, to its supremacy, which hardly makes him a likely candidate for materialism. His 'materialism' was simply his belief in a providential universe, open to man's understanding and control, a belief not new with Temple of course, but implicit in Christian doctrines from Paul onwards, and Temple saw this as leading to a concern for and understanding of both 'matter' and 'flesh', rather than as hatred of the spirit for them. Indeed if he had used the word 'flesh' rather than 'mind' his stand would have been clearer, for he was thinking incarnationally. His unfortunate aphorism simply did damage to a creed which was sacramental — that spirit poured grace upon matter, so transforming it, which was for him almost a definition of Art, to which indeed he gave that capital letter.

There was a lot to be said for materialism (in the philosophic sense) in my youth. If one accepted a Newtonian

[1] Macmillan 1934, p. 478.
[2] Op. cit., p. 488.

75

universe of impenetrable and indeed incomprehensible atoms subject to motion, to attraction and repulsion, it seemed indeed, as Hobbes said, as though this had to be the final answer to everything. If these tough, inert little bricks of the universe worked in these ways, formed these patterns, created these galaxies, what could we do? It seemed irresistible as a metaphysic and so pervasive in nineteenth-century philosophy that the only answer seemed to be to deny matter any reality and lodge everything in the mind (or Mind, as Temple would say), which was the idealists' position. The trouble was that if one became a materialist in that absolute sense then everything which was human, every single thing which made human life glorious and tragic and gave it meaning — belief and love, sacrifice, genius, or death — was emptied of all content. We were phantoms, no more: the stuff dreams were made of, as a wiser man said. It was this which made materialism of the strict metaphysical sort unendurable, an anaemia of the human spirit.

But as the century has advanced the materialism which was a product of the earlier physicists' view of the universe has perished: the physicists themselves are guilty of the infanticide:

> Nature and Nature's laws, lay hid in night:
> God said, *let Newton be*! and all was light —

But as J. C. Squire said to Alexander Pope;

> It did not last: the Devil, howling *Ho*!
> *Let Einstein be*! restored the status quo.

The sociologists continue to talk of the demystification of the world as the source of its secularization. But the physicists have certainly remystified matter. Its solidity, impenetrability and independence have all gone in what appears to the layman to be an infinite recession of particles of fractional life indistinguishable from flashes of energy. We even have anti-matter: the theory of matter devouring matter: concepts of time-reversal: the notion of a universe exploding into being and moving to some appointed end eluding human understanding. This is so very far from the notion of a universe transparent to the intellect, the laws of whose operation would one day be totally known, that one is awed by the metaphysical transformation which has overtaken our times and which gives a dated look to all those debates of my youth.

If, however, even for Temple, though he did not know it, the Materialism to which he gave a capital M was already dead, the moral sort was not. It was often enough used, even in its metaphysical heyday, in a pejorative sense and still is. When we speak today of a materialist society, or philosophy, we are thinking, not of Newton, but of attitudes of greed, of selfishness, of moral indifference, of hostility to everything except worldly possessions and sensual satisfactions. That is one reason why Temple's aphorism could only be totally misunderstood today.

For me, as that young man finding his way, materialism, as a metaphysical creed, posed an aesthetic problem. Or to put it another way, I wanted to get at the metaphysical problem standing behind the aesthetic dilemma. When in the thirties I fell so ill and rested for weeks under the pear tree in the garden of the kindly house which German bombs were subsequently to blow up, I used to carry a portable wireless set onto the lawn. For the first time in my life I had the leisure to listen to music, and had so deep a hunger for it that I felt that without it I should never recover. The B.B.C. was passing through one of its Bach phases, and cantatas, choral preludes, unaccompanied partitas — like the Sonata No. 4 in D Minor which included the Chaconne which Menuhin played so exquisitely — flooded the air, not all understood or appreciated by my untrained ear, but pregnant with the messages of a universe Newton had not sought to describe and which I had now to try to understand.

The meaning of music baffled me. Speech has a certain concreteness which can be intellectually handled: to certain sounds precise objects or states can be attached — 'dog', 'cat', 'hunger' and 'thirst'. Music lacks this: the effort to produce a synthetic concreteness results only in dull programme music. Yet music was not, because of this, unintellectual or anti-intellectual. It was a statement above the level of intellect. If it was a communication of the most profound sort, not in strictly intellectual terms, then I had also to ask — to what part of me was it addressed? It was useless to reply — the emotional: for what was the *me* which loved, hated and feared and had so many other unstable feelings, the source and power of which were often beyond 'my' control or understanding? It was a problem which pressed heavily on the materialist. On the materialist plane tickling one's ear with sounds ought to have the same importance that tickling one's feet with a feather had. 'Pushpin was as good as poetry,' that fatuous old man Jeremy Bentham had once said. But if, just for the sake of hypothesis, one admitted the existence of an entity called 'spirit', then one could admit immediately communications, such as music and poetry, of spirit to spirit. One could make sense of it all only by ceasing to be materialist. But if one ceased to be a materialist, what then? Where intellectually was one's resting place? I had come gradually deeply to distrust those who went around arrogantly proclaiming their materialism and their atheism, yet imported into their hard creed all sorts of ideas intolerable within it — as that there ought to be justice in the world, and freedom of speech and conscience, and self-development for every child. How could materialism contain *a moral ought*? How could it talk so loosely about 'the spirit' of man, of civilization, of mercy, or of anything else?

In music I had pursued spiritual realities to their source, time and time again, in the liturgies of Christianity. Music contained the most tremendous humanist and Christian statements. How my friends used to praise Bach's Mass in B Minor! How often I heard it discussed, or read of it! There seemed to be a conspiracy to think of it as pure music, divorced from human or social reality. I felt like the Marxists about it, and often longed to say 'but surely the whole point about it is that it is an act of most devout worship?' But if I dared to say so, no one seemed to regard it as significant: my remark was received in silence, as though it were a social *faux pas*. The art was valid: the faith on which it was based was dismissed as irrelevant. This made so little sense to me that I felt the exact opposite: if the art was valid, then surely in some sense the belief must be valid too? If one revered the flowering of the human spirit through centuries of European history, could one so easily dismiss the soil of faith in which it grew?

Yet when one stated this one faced a second contemporary conspiracy — to dismiss religion except in an anthropological sense as unworthy of the serious attention of modern man.

78

To do this, the intellectuals had to avert their faces and pretend that Max Weber and R.H. Tawney did not really exist, of course, but were merely a rumour. They were Comteans to a man. One could discuss religion in a hostile way, from a position of superiority, but not sympathetically. To admit the possibility of belief in it was rather like supposing that witches flew on broomsticks: it was primitive, dead, abandoned by modern man. The great laugh was the Tennessee 'monkey' trial over the teaching of evolution. That a civilization had grown out of Christianity and owed all its presuppositions to it merely raised incredulous eyebrows. It could not be true, we thought. We were, in the twenties and thirties, very much the blinkered products of our little day.

PART THREE

Where was, in what Abyss, my Speaking Tongue?
THOMAS TRAHERNE

1

Marx and Freud, my mentors, dismissed religion out of hand. For Freud it was a neurosis, the projection of the powerful father figure of our infancy on to the skies to continue there to haunt and tyrannize over us with his castration threats. He found nothing in God but, in Sir William Watson's words, 'man's giant shadow, hailed divine.' At least that was so until his discovery of a death impulse in man, a magnet in him which turned him against his will to that total extinction which death promised every man and the expectation of which grew behind every man's thoughts and fears, no matter how powerful or fulfilled he was, until what was feared and expected became what he hungered for. How else end all his griefs and frustrations? Freud never knew the profundity of his discovery. It made his Oedipus—castration—complex childish by comparison. For the castration threat was pure fantasy, infantile in every sense, for fathers do not in the normal way emasculate their sons, not even the stern Victorian types that Freud lived among and from which limited sample he deduced so much. But all men died. All men had to die. This is what every man once he is in full consciousness sees ahead of him. This is the final reality, and in the hands of atheist Freud the most profound religious discovery!

If Marx had been a Freudian, all fathers would have had to be capitalists and all sons proletarians and then honour would have been satisfied. But Marx would have been happy with Freud's bourgeois fathers. He was one himself. And, for Marx, the striking thing was that, socially, religious structures and teachings supported the social order (as for Freud they supported the sexual order). So religion appeared a soporific, if not exactly invented by the bourgeoisie (it almost came to that) then certainly exploited by them to keep the workers quiet — the famous 'opium of the people', a force that stood in the way of revolution.

In the passage in which he produced that still reverberating phrase he also said, 'Man makes religion, religion does not make man' — an interesting echo of Jesus's 'The Sabbath is made for man, not man for the Sabbath' — and went on,

Religion is indeed man's self-consciousness and self-awareness as long as he has not found his feet in the universe. But man is not an abstract being, squatting outside the world. Man is the world of men, the State, and society. *This State, this society, produce religion* which is an inverted world consciousness, because they are an inverted world. Religion is the general theory of this world, its encyclopaedic compendium, its logic in popular form, its spiritual *point d'honneur*, its enthusiasm, its moral sanction, its solemn complement, its general basis of consolation and justification. It is the fantastic realization of the human being. Religious suffering is at the same time an expression of real suffering and a protest against real suffering. Religion is the sigh of the oppressed creature, the sentiment of a heartless world, and the soul of soulless conditions.[1] (My italics.)

With so much lyrically to be said in praise of Christianity it is a wonder Marx could not have gone farther and seen religion as a protest *against* the bourgeois order too and the world might then have been spared much suffering and Marxism itself its spiritual desiccation. For the bourgeois order was the first in European history in which religion came seriously under atheistic attack, religious orders dispersed, priests and nuns murdered and *State* propaganda could be directed against religion, and churches rendered impotent. (I am thinking mainly of the French revolution onwards.) Under that order politicians, writers, poets, editors, professors could be atheists or agnostics, hostile to the faith of multitudes of humbler peoples who depended on them. Indeed, under the Marquis de Sade and his many followers not only religion, but morality too, became dispensable.

Marx, who argued for the total identification of the bourgeoisie and capitalism (and this, too, was a fatal mistake), saw nevertheless in the bourgeois order something new and destructive let loose on the world. In a too often ignored hymn to the revolutionary bourgeoisie in *The Communist Manifesto*, he wrote:

---

[1] *Marx-Engels Gesamtausgabe* 1/1/1, from *Karl Marx, Selected Writings*, ed. T.B. Bottomore and M. Rubel. Pelican 1963.

The bourgeoisie . . . has pitilessly torn asunder the motley feudal ties that bound man to his 'natural superiors', and has left remaining no other nexus between man and man than naked self-interest, than callous 'cash payment'. It has drowned the most heavenly ecstasies of religious fervour, of chivalrous enthusiasm, of philistine sentimentalism, in the icy water of egotistical calculation. . . . The bourgeoisie has stripped of its halo every occupation hitherto honoured and looked up to with reverent awe. It has converted the physician, the lawyer, the priest, the poet, the man of science, into its paid wage-labourers . . . has reduced the family relation to a mere money relation. . . . It has accomplished wonders . . . (it) cannot exist without constantly revolutionizing . . .[2]

And so the paean goes on. And had he been as clairvoyant of the bourgeois future as he had been clearsighted about its past he could have added that it would be the bourgeois who would make the proletarian revolutions against the bourgeois, providing the theories, the policies, the leaders, the eloquent denunciations of oppression, the thick, fat academic tomes, the godless lust for power, just as he, Karl Marx, eminent bourgeois scholar, was to do for the whole of his life. The explosive, destructive bourgeois turned its revolutionary dynamic against itself. And when it won, the triumphant younger sons of the bourgeoisie, 'in the name of the proletariat', turned their backs on all that daring and demonism which had transformed the world (and created *them*), and restored the feudal rule of superior persons. An intellectual ice age was imposed lest the grandsons should be infected with that old bourgeois revolutionary spirit to the detriment of their fathers.

If we need to bring Freud into it we could point to the irony, which somehow escaped him, that the revolutionary sons did not need to kill the old man, only to castrate him. But with the sons genitally intact the bourgeois could survive, or some of them, even the most revolutionary age. Only the contemporary generation has come to see the post-renaissance explosion of learning, rather than the acquisition of money,

---

[2] First published 1848. Translated by Samuel Moore and revised by Friedrich Engels.

as the true bourgeois weapon in the destruction of the old world.

Well, there it was, the attack on religion was as important to Marxism as its attack on capitalism. I am not sure it could distinguish between the two, hamstrung as it was by its cultural determinism. The ineptitude of its analysis had become as painful to me in the thirties as the callowness of Freud's diagnosis of a religious neurosis from which men stood in need of a cure as if it were a fetishist disease like cutting off the pigtails of little girls. So colossal, so arrogant a dismissal of man's everlasting longing for answers to his questions about his nature and destiny would better have come from morose adolescents than men of science and humanity.

I could only feel contempt in the thirties for the superficiality of contemporary attacks on religion. If I could not be a thorough-going materialist where was there a resting place for mind or spirit short of religion? Most of my contemporaries were not thorough-going materialists: they flinched from so merciless a creed. But they were not religious either. They imported into a vague religiosity a materialist content: or sprinkled over their materialism a holy water of idealism. Even the Marxists were idealist-materialists (dragging in Hegel to support Haeckel).

2

I worked for my father in Fleet Street (it was the second run) from 1924 to 1929. What he paid during those years was so inadequate (thirty shillings — and never increased) that I had to look around for other sources of income. The local authorities paid for some classes I took in literature for members of the Woodcraft Folk, and the editors of the various papers my father represented began to lean more and more on me for news coverage of a special sort and for book reviews. Scores of books began to pass through my hands. I could be lavish with presents. I enjoyed hammering what I thought were bad books and collecting those I thought were good. I began to write to publishers for those I specially wanted to review. At the same time I was writing furiously for myself and getting things into various journals, including poems in *The Observer, Good Housekeeping*(!) and left-wing reviews. I had a book of poems published in 1927 and my first full-length book, *The Folk Trail*, published by Noel Douglas in 1929. I wrote another book at the same time about tramping and camping in the spring through the south-west of England and crossing Dartmoor by the leats and through the bogs, but though it was liked by publishers *Southwards and Westwards* never got published and the manuscript is lost. This is one early book I should like to see again. Whatever else I was doing those days — and founding and running the Woodcraft Folk was the most important of them — I was writing continually and setting the discipline for a life of authorship. Indeed, the money I was earning from writing was becoming more important than the weekly alleged wage from my father but somehow I was too inept and self-effacing even to try to capitalize on all this and get myself a staff job somewhere. *The Peterborough Advertiser* was prepared to take me on as a staff reporter *in Peterborough*. But how could I leave the youth movement I was building up in London? Besides I was desperately in love.

I loathed my father's style of life. Running a newspaper, or writing for one, was fine, but cadging for advertisements was a degrading occupation. To succeed one had to exude a nauseating *bonhomie* with the revolting creatures advertising then produced and, boozy oneself, win from the boozier what they would never concede when sober. How often as a boy I had hung around in the rain outside pub doors waiting for my father to come out, consoled, if he remembered at all, by a biscuit and a lemonade thrust through the glass doors. He would apologize to my misery, saying he had been seeing clients. All that life was totally alien to the life-style we sought in our puritanical youth movement.

The break came in the spring of 1929. My father was to lose his two principal newspapers through amalgamation. I could see there would be no place for me in the few provincial papers he would have left — *The Peterborough Advertiser, The Boston Guardian, The Worcester Echo* and so forth — and that in any case they would not bring him in enough to keep him in his expensive masonic style of life. He had never had the sense to sign a contract with his principal dailies which would compel them to grant him dismissal compensation. He was offered a job with Northcliffe Newspapers which his pride failed to recognize as a new, clean start. He could only think he would be earning a quarter of his previous income. Besides, his despairing alcoholism was fast overwhelming him, no matter how the family battled for his soul. He was losing the capacity for any kind of job, for any kind of decision. Perhaps he saw my desertion as yet another betrayal. He was in his quiet way both proud and distrustful of my literary abilities. Perhaps it gave him assurance to say, 'My son will attend to that,' or 'My son wrote that,' and this helped his sanity. It cannot have been easy to say to his boozy friends, 'My son has left me,' when his whole world was leaving him. But what was I to do? Experienced men were getting unemployed by the dozen in Fleet Street just then. I, at twenty-three, was a boy, a mere nothing with no future and no qualifications.

My exit was hastened by a freak commission. Dr William Brown, the Harley Street psychiatrist, and no less than Wilde Reader of Mental Philosophy at Oxford, had been asked to deliver six lectures on 'Mind and Body' at the Savoy Hill studios of the B.B.C. Eminent though he was, he was not very fluent with his pen and I was engaged by him, through the offices of a friend, to write his lectures for him. So, free of Fleet Street, I went week by week to his Harley Street consulting rooms, talked about his attitudes to Freud and Jung, Rivers and McDougall and went home, armed with a bag of books and papers and wrote each specimen talk which we then worked over together until we shaped it to represent his views. I then took the talk to the B.B.C. producer and we tested it for length. At the same time I wrote the B.B.C. booklet to advertise the lecture series, even drawing, quite professionally, the neurones, synapses, sections through the spinal column which the booklet text demanded! The talks took place in November and December 1929. The booklet sold (I was told) three million copies! Just my luck that the bestseller of my life does not bear my name anywhere. It was followed by a number of other commissions from Dr Brown and the B.B.C. which saw me frugally, but pleasantly, through 1929 and 1930. But in February 1930 my father had a stroke from which he never recovered consciousness. He was only fifty, my mother fifty-four. To my precarious freelancing was now added the responsibility of a widowed mother and two very small children: life was as accident prone as ever, you see, for I was hard put just to survive myself. Dr William Brown had faded from the scene after I had written his piece for *The New Learning*. Nothing after all had come of my bee-like sips at the nectar of scholarship in Harley Street and Oxford. It is true that Dr Brown offered me a lectureship in psychology at the University of London. 'But I do not even have matriculation,' I said. That ended the conversation.

In 1931 I headed a Co-operative delegation to the U.S.S.R. Acting as party leader reduced the cost to me to almost nil (but even that nil I had to borrow). It was the rage just then to write travel accounts of Russia and I prudently saw newspapers and journals before I left and arranged to write stories for them about Russia when I returned. We were away nearly two months and our first intimation of disaster was when we dropped off at Hamburg, where Nazis and Commies and police were fighting in the streets and we found the bank doors permanently closed. When we got to Leningrad we learnt of the crisis at home, the economic blizzard, the destruction of the Labour Government and the formation of the National Government under Ramsay MacDonald. When we returned from that extended tour, blight had settled on England. No one wanted my Russian experiences. The material I had collected, together with statistics assiduously gathered from a multitude of sources, eventually made a book on the Consumer Co-operatives of the U.S.S.R. (*Co-operation in the U.S.S.R.*, 1934) but alas, the *only* book, for the consumer movement in Russia was abolished by party decree soon after the publication of my survey (so another door closed). I showed Sidney Webb my material before it was published and he said he did not think it would make a book. It did, and he borrowed its statistics for his vainglorious compendium *Soviet Communism: a New Civilization* published a year later. I am encapsulated in footnotes there.

To retrieve my fortunes I sat down and wrote an auto-biographical novel, published in 1932 as *Fugitive Morning* by a new, inexperienced publisher Denis Archer. What a press it received! The scores and scores of reviews filled a cuttings book. It got mentioned several times on the radio. 'So good,

89

so natural, so sincere and so courageous,' said Gerald Gould in the *Observer*. 'Has a sustained note of real beauty running through it,' said the *Saturday Review* and the *New Statesman* exclaimed, 'It is a kind of unsophisticated *Portrait of an Artist* with the addition of Ian Hay humour . . . an exciting experience.' Even *The Times Literary Supplement*, august with anonymity, said 'Mr Paul really does know the boy mind, and he is wholly sincere in setting down his knowledge with honesty and frankness . . . unusually well executed,' while Geoffrey West in the *Adelphi* described it as 'totally admirable'. Many Sunday newspapers and reviews assessed it among 'Books of the Year' in December 1932. The *Tatler*, the *Sketch* and the *Illustrated London News* carried my photograph. What *established* author would not have welcomed such laudation? I was certain that my name and income were assured. Alas, it sold only 365 copies and my second novel, begun with the wildest hopes, *Periwake*, a Wellsian story of an unemployed little man from the suburbs, was published with the gloomiest expectations and did not sell either despite selection by the Book Guild and headlines in the *News Chronicle*. It was a doomed book: due to appear in translation in Vienna on 3rd September 1939 with Saturn-Verlag, the war swept it away. It was not surprising that in the face of all these struggles and disasters I fell ill, beaten to my knees, and only survived by building up a teaching connection in the evening literary and other institutes of the London County Council and the Workers' Educational Association. This work eventually filled my life – exhaustingly too, for I might have twelve two-hour sessions a week at places as far apart as Erith, Tottenham and Morden, travelling everywhere by bus and tram and train. This left me only Fridays and Saturdays to write my weekly articles or do my broadcasts, and Sundays to sleep. I resigned from leadership of the Woodcraft Folk but remained a working president. What saved my sanity was that the evening institutes shut down for two months in the summer and for about a month at Christmas and Easter. I was then unpaid, of course.

How then did I manage to find the time to get involved in the Social Democratic underground in Austria after the rise of Dollfuss to power? I find myself incredulous. I had strong personal connections with the Austrian Social Democrats and their Red Falcon children's movement through my friendship with the delightful, cultivated Anton Tesarek, a school teacher, founder of the Falcons, and his wife Reserl and son Till. We exchanged visits continually and Till, a close personal friend — now a psychiatrist in Vienna — was as much at home with the Woodcraft Folk in Britain as in his own Red Falcons in Vienna. Through Tesarek I came to be a member of the Austrian underground, familiar with his own cell, crossing into Czechoslovakia to meet other underground leaders and to discuss and consult and, as a kind of courier, bringing in and taking out material of an illegal kind in my journeys to and from England. It was particularly important to carry out the passports and valuables of those about to escape documentless over the Swiss frontier. All this work was intensified after Hitler came to power, and was brought to an end only by the outbreak of war. At the end of the war, while serving in Palestine, I received a card, written in indelible pencil, and many times redirected, from Anton Tesarek. He had been released by the American Forces from the death quarries. On first arrest he had been beaten up many times to confess to his association with the spy Leslie Paul. He now wanted to be cleared before the American authorities, and was, of course, before I could help him. In a recent publication, *Notizen aus Einem Tugebuch* (1975), Anton spoke of my 'courageous, carefree and sacrificial help' to the Austrian underground. I simply enjoyed it. I was gratified to find that most of my fears were in my imagination. In the presence of actual danger I was cool and unafraid and full of presence of mind. But I was not tested very severely.

It was through these links that I brought out a brilliant Viennese boy pianist, Walter Wagner, a Jew, and after that from Austria and Czechoslovakia something like thirty or forty Jewish, Catholic, and Social Democratic children whose families were threatened. We placed them with British working-class families, and meeting up with one of them in Rochdale a year after his placement and asking, 'Wie gehts, Franz?' I received the reply, 'Eh, champion!'

I became a member of the breakaway 'Neu Beginnen',[3] a

---

[3] Cf. *Socialism's New Start*: a secret German manifesto by 'Miles', preface by H.N. Brailsford. N.C.L.C. 1934.

German Social Democratic splinter group which, shocked into existence by the raging, triumphant success of the Nazi revolution, now questioned everything – the basic theorems of Marxism, the readiness of the working class for revolution, the capacity of Communist and Social Democratic Marxists for reliable historical analysis, the future of Labour. It argued the case for the 'bourgeoisification' of the western working classes long before anyone else had seen this and pointed to the unreliability of the Russian Communist Party, to its nationalism and to its terror as an instrument totally alien to the socialist spirit. These were the years of the purges, the Nazi-Communist alliance to defeat the Social Democratic government of Prussia, the lying popular fronts, the massacre of Russian peasantry, the Spanish Civil War, and finally of the alliance between Stalin and Hitler. They demanded a reassessment in depth, in anguish, of one's intellectual and spiritual allegiances. And so my own spiritual turmoil began again and had to be fought through in the face of a great deal of illness.

It was typical of my increasing cynicism in the thirties that I wrote a long satire, *Crissake*. It was a kind of *Candide*, a poor relation. The title was deliberately blasphemous. H.G. Wells had written somewhere about the exasperated idiots who, rather than think, said, 'For crissake let's do somethink.' I took 'Crissake' for my hero's name. He went through a series of adventures which entangled him in succession with every movement of the day. As I was editor of *Plan*, the review of the Federation of Progressive Societies and Individuals, I knew all the movements from the loony to the lovable. Crissake begins at school with the Crusaders and the Oxford Groupers and dubious initiations into pederasty and, after fascism, spiritualism, occultism, nudism, freesexism and heaven knows what, ends up as a fervent highly placed communist in the Red Square, Moscow (prophetic, that bit, anticipating Burgess, Philby, Maclean and others whose evolution was not dissimilar) cheering Stalin as he passed. To prove himself a thorough Muscovite he is also learning to chew sunflower seeds and spit out the husks. But he is inept. The husks hit Stalin in the eye. Crissake is arrested and tried in a show trial on an assassination attempt directed at the divine leader by a devilish imperialist-Jewish-capitalist-left-deviationist-fascist plot against the classless-peace-loving-workers' homeland of the U.S.S.R. If that was not the end of Crissake, it deserved to be. The manuscript rests in the vaults of Texas University from which may it never be resurrected. At least it showed how deep my disillusion went. After *Crissake* I could not write fiction for many years.

My poetry was also in ruins. Looking back, I can see the point of the very first book, published when I was twenty-one, of which a portion appears above on pp. 69-70. It was artless, enthusiastic, word-drunk, polemical in an adolescent way —

> God is in his heaven
> And Mammon on his throne,
> Old men rejoicing
> And youth turned to stone.

— but it showed a Whitmanesque passion and ability to get some reality down on paper. But I did not recognize this ability in myself and *A Green Love* (1931) is unreadable. It has all the vices of that high-flown poetical poetry of the Georgians with none of their homely virtues.

> Should poets bicycle-pump the human heart
> Or squash it flat?

Kingsley Amis once asked. I was bicycle-pumping like mad.

My little book derived from the anthology *The Open Road* and *The Week-end Book* rather than those deeper, pessimistic instincts, that feeling for realism, which surfaced later. It was sentimental, gushing, uncritical and might have been written by a spinster teacher in Bognor. St John Adcock was right when he said that it showed a determination to write rather than poetry itself. I was overwhelmed by my dislike of the book almost as soon as it was published. The flaw of sentimentality in me that I now detected seemed to be fatal to the kind of writer I aspired to be. I feared I had infected the Woodcraft Folk with it and that it governed my relations with other people and with the children of the movement. It was partly to rid myself of this emotional dishonesty that I had written my novel about the General Strike (in which I had participated as a strike leader), *Men in May*, which

Gollancz published in 1936, just too ·early, of course, to catch the market of the Left Book Club. I suppose *Crissake*, which followed it, owed a lot to my rage against sentimentalism, my new hatred of gush. There were other bad literary models before me, besides the Georgian anthologies and those illustrated poetry sheets we bought from The Poetry Bookshop — 'Time you old gypsy man' and 'O blackbird what a boy you are!' and so on — to decorate our rooms. Lawrence was a fatal influence, for he was a sentimental writer too: his poetry trembled on the verge of it. *Sons and Lovers* was of the realism I had striven for in *Fugitive Morning*, but *Lady Chatterley's Lover*, which I had bought in Paris and smuggled back with *Ulysses*, oozed with it on almost every page. But those were the years when it was obligatory (especially for the Federation of Progressive Societies) to accept the genius of Lawrence uncritically, and to praise the mush. *Lady Chatterley's Lover* today reads like a book by a man who had never had sexual intercourse, but only imagined it. But *Sons and Lovers* is superb.

Feeling my writing career at an end I stopped writing books in 1937, resigned to thinking of my future only in terms of teaching in adult education. The imminence of war with, as I and my friends expected, the destruction of European civilization and ourselves as well, was in any case a great discouragement. I was not to publish another book for six years, and that, *The Annihilation of Man*, was grim enough not only in title but in its analysis of the disaster which had overtaken Europe. As to poetry, I published no volume again until 1951 — nearly twenty years after the last. I select two poems, one from *Exile and Other Poems* (1951) and the other from *Journey to Connemara and Other Poems* (1972), to show that after the thirties I redeemed the promise I made to myself as a boy of thirteen, leaning against a lamp post waiting for a tram at the end of a long desolate war, to be a poet.

POEM

The night is dark as still water
Imprisoning yet not dissolving all
Making fluid only the fringes
Of adamant earth.

I know but cannot see
The thin walls, the staring windows,
The undulating droop of curtains
And beyond the sightless grass
Lean topheavy trees
Closed flowers unmoving.

Dawn is a knife edge under the stone
Of night, a long cold thrust,
A rending away.
I feel earth like a swimmer
Rolling and rising from drowned
Depths to the aerate, leaping
Chrysolite sea.

My window an eye now.
The ash a vague heap of nothing
Tumbling over the sky.
Now all the little friendly lights
Are come again
Bare undersides of leaves
Steel tips to grass
Wet pavings, silken roads,
Roofs molten slate.

Morning makes strange the curtain ripples
Sparks with revealing light the plumy
Dark of bottles, books and chairs
And in fathomless feathers winnowing shade
Uncovers in first creation, you,
Marbled, dear and unknown.

The eyes beside me are strange
Deep sunken pockets still,
The throat a hollow cave.
I think you are dead
When you sleep thus and would
Hurl the steely blades of light
To pierce and wake you beside me
Warm when you sleep thus dark dear
Unmoving like the dead
When day is come.

My second poem, which first appeared in *The Contemporary Review*, concerns Simone Weil, who, like me, worked her passage back from Marxism to Christianity during the war years. She died of starvation in Grosvenor Sanatorium, Ashford, Kent, a voluntary death which the Coroner recorded as suicide because she refused to eat more than the minimum ration allowed to the occupied French even though she was also terminally ill with tuberculosis. When I was Director of Studies at Brasted Place College one of my students, doing a study of her, stumbled on the fact that she was buried in a pauper's grave. I at once, in collaboration with E.W.F. Tomlin of the British Council, launched an appeal through *The Times* to have a memorial placed on her grave. To make this possible and to prevent anyone being buried on top of her, I bought her grave, which I still own.

LADY WHOSE GRAVE I OWN
(for Simone Weil, died 1943)

Ah Simone, was it love of God that struck you down,
Or the more compelling love of men?
There is an affliction of the body too,
   which trembles in the eyes,
In the palm's sweat, the straight but straying hair,
Unguarded tongue and makes unlovely
That which loves with such a fever
The body's broken by a rigor.
If you had loved less, cared less!
Caring and loving all
Made certain that slow fall.

Simone, I know the Martha tribe that labours
Down the years to win reward,
The washing-up that has polemical intent,
Twice-scrubbed floors: knitting feverish against
The too-late hours; the sullen glance through misted
   spectacles
That hungers for and mulishly rejects the cherished word
Thinking — if you do not see my works are love,
Get out of my way. I'm just a doormat for you.

There can be too much urgency to give of love.
Those workman's boots and graceless jumpers
The endless cigarettes and rough political debates
The redflag marches on the local Mairie,
That mastery of Sophocles and Marx
Spoke of another hunger than — give my brilliant wit the
   floor:
The panic flight of mind, the long night's fever
That there was only age and barrenness ahead.

It is a sad thing that so much we carry in our hearts and
   hands,
Gifts profligate on our poor shoulders
Are soon like broken things rejected. What point
In birth and growing and eager learning
If there is no human answer to our burning?
But was it for prams and nightie promiscuity
Pomaded Paris husband and the marital tiff
Bourgeois sons in love with their moustaches
You really longed?
Or the Promethean task
The North-West passage of the bruised and hungry soul?

(This is my body: is it given for me?)

It is the mark of the afflicted that
Their own sin's endurable
But they carry into heartbreak
The burden of another's pain,
And more, they are all gravity,
So stricken
Beyond all earthly hope is their despair.

The complacency of the unafflicted
Is more than they can stomach
The adolescent sniggers, the casual lovers
In shadowed arcades, the faceless men in faultless suits
In the Kremlins of power.

And so, Simone, lady whose grave I own,
The migraine, the nausea without cessation,

97

The Solesmes masses beating on the brain,
The iron will to shrug off so much suffering —
This we know
                    But tell us godly Simone
Of the waiting till the Saviour came again.

Was this the real affliction,
The cross you had to bear,
That you were simply what you were?

I discovered T.S. Eliot in the thirties with the same excitement that I had come across Whitman some years earlier.
Eliot struck me with astonishment: he is familiar enough
now, but then he was a revolution. He wrote in crisp images
of urban life which left me breathless, for here was the
smoky London I knew, even to the cabhorses:

Of restless nights in one-night cheap hotels
And sawdust restaurants with oyster shells

The yellow fog that rubs its back upon the window-panes

With a bald spot in the middle of my hair

I grow old . . .   I grow old . . .
I shall wear the bottoms of my trousers rolled

A lonely cabhorse steams and stamps
And then the lighting of the lamps.

              . . . the damp souls of housemaids
Sprouting despondently at area gates.

It was not just the accuracy of Eliot's observation of urban
life, which was my life, which was so important, but his sheer
nerve in making lines of poetry out of:

It's them pills I took, to bring it off, she said
(She's had five already, and nearly died of young George.)

Here was poetry of a vastly different calibre from Brooke's
'rose-crowned into the darkness' or 'Breathless we flung
us on the windy hill' or all that business of nightingales
and roses and country cottages beloved of the pre-1914 poets

98

especially — though there were many in the twenties for whom poetry was only poetry if it disinfected and deodorized life with honeysuckle spray.

Then too I had come to know and reverence the war poets — Sassoon with his tanks lurching down the stalls and scarlet majors short of breath. He could write such quickening lines as:

Everyone suddenly burst out singing:
And I was filled with such delight
As prisoned birds must find in freedom
Winging wildly across the white
Orchards and dark green fields; on; on;
    and out of sight.

or Wilfred Owen:

What passing bells for those who die as cattle?
Only the monstrous anger of the guns
Only the stuttering rifles' rapid rattle
Can patter out their hasty orisons.

or again, from 'Dulce et Decorum Est', this realism:

Gas! Gas! Quick, boys — An ecstasy of fumbling,
Fitting the clumsy helmets just in time,
But someone still was yelling out and stumbling
and flound'ring like a man in fire or lime.

In the face of all that how could I write so long ago (in *A Green Love*)

But Oh! My love was like a song to which
    The suns went shouting while earth span to seek
The flowers I heaped, for flowers sang like larks
    And I never knew what spring was till I heard you speak.

So much bad Chesterton, worse Brooke! There were harder lessons to come with the advent of the thirties' poets, Auden and Spender, Day Lewis, Louis MacNeice, William Empson and others, some of whom, indeed, I was to publish in *Plan*. It was often, self-consciously, poetry of the struggle of the times. In Auden's (subsequently suppressed) 'Spain':

To-morrow, perhaps the future. The research on fatigue
And the movements of packers: the gradual exploring of all the
      Octaves of radiation;
To-morrow the enlarging of consciousness by diet and
  breathing.
  . . .
To-morrow the hour of the pageant-master and the musician,

The beautiful roar of the chorus under the dome:
To-morrow the exchanging of tips on the breeding of terriers,
      The eager election of chairmen
By the sudden forest of hands. But to-day the struggle.

Almost all of those poets, despite their superficial communism, with its official optimism about human history, were filled with just that kind of foreboding about the future, about the fragility of civilization, the infinite corruptibility of man, the tenuousness of human relations. They saw man, as I was beginning to do in the thirties, as 'poised between shocking falls on razor-edge' and teaching himself, as a disguise, 'the balancing subterfuges'. For the war poets *war* was the unaccountable disaster: for the poets of the thirties it was *man*. We are already in the world of Sartrian bad faith and the angry isolation of Kierkegaardian existentialism! 'Doom is dark and deeper than any sea-dingle,' wrote Auden and we applied it to ourselves and our times. Another phrase of his, 'gradual ruin spreading like a stain', burnt on our minds like acid. It was not only the depression of the West we had in mind, but the rise of Hitler and what was leaking out about Stalin's Russia (despite the drooling adulation of Shaw and the Webbs). I myself in my lectures from 1932 onwards was prophesying another world war within a decade, engineered by Germany. I published a pamphlet, *Blood and Soil*, which I translated from French and German to show the war intentions of the Nazis. Sometimes I was mobbed for my pains. 'Capitalists will never make war on capitalists again,' my communist students shouted at me. 'But you'll see they'll all combine against the Soviet Union, the workers' fatherland!'

Yet another mood was discernible in the thirties' poetry beside the revolutionary and existentialist tones. It was of sadness, even despair. Just to recognize this was to see how far the poet had moved in a hundred years or so from his role

100

as official optimist about man, his laureate post as the unacknowledged legislator of mankind.

> I thank whatever gods may be
> For my unconquerable soul. (Henley)

or

> To suffer woes which Hope thinks infinite:
> To forgive wrongs darker than death or night:
>   To defy Power, which seems omnipotent;
> To love, and bear; to hope till Hope creates
> From its own wreck the thing it contemplates:
>   Neither to change, nor falter, nor repent;
> This, like thy glory, Titan, is to be
> Good, great and joyous, beautiful and free:
> This is alone life, Joy, Empire and Victory.
>
> (Shelley)

But Auden wrote:

> For poetry makes nothing happen: it survives
> In the valley of its saying where executives
> Would never want to tamper; it flows south
> From the ranches of isolation and the busy griefs,
> Past towns that we believe and die in: it survives
> A way of happening, a mouth.
>   ('In memory of W.B. Yeats')

A mouth! No longer, you see, *a song*! The poets could no longer believe in their own poetry. This was their own unhappy mood in the thirties in the face of the Freudian and Marxist critiques of the arts and the taste of approaching disaster in the wind.

> What is that sound high in the air
> Murmurs of maternal lamentation
> Who are those hooded hordes swarming
> Over endless plains, stumbling in cracked earth . . .
>   ('The Waste Land')

and Eliot even redefined man in the scarecrow image:

> We are the hollow men
> We are the stuffed men
> Leaning together
> Headpiece filled with straw. Alas!

101

'The Hollow Men' is haunted with sibilance like a gigantic sigh. 'Piece', 'straw', 'voices', 'grass', 'glass', 'Rat's coat, crowskin, crossed staves', 'Falls the Shadow'. The sibilance is ghostly, itself a shadow falling across all Eliot's poetry, an exhalation from the soul of man. Something is said in those hisses about his vast disappointment with Prufrock humanity, lost in the smoke and fog of the December afternoons of his earlier urban poetry which is characterized by simple acceptance of the human condition so that one need only know it, taste it, without approaching it first through ideological blinkers. I gave lectures in which I tried to trace the growing sibilance of Eliot's poetry through to his plays and the *Four Quartets*. I had in mind Marx's definition of religion as the sigh of the world (one point where that angry old man reached out to poetry). For Eliot it was certainly one long, hesitant, humble breath, unmistakable when he read his poetry aloud as plainsong, as an incantation, as he did to a group of us, at my request, in Jerusalem Chambers.

For Thine is
Life is
For Thine is the

answered in 'Ash Wednesday':

Till the wind shakes a thousand whispers from the yew.
And after this our exile.

I never completed my study of the significance of this sibilance — it began to seem too precious — but it colours my love and understanding of Eliot and I am glad that he became a friend after the Second War. D.S. Savage in *The Personal Principle* argued that the loss (in the *Four Quartets* for instance) of that vivid urban imagery characteristic of Eliot's earlier poetry was the loss of poetry itself. But poetry is hydra-headed. I could always see the value of philosophic poetry stripped of imagery even to bareness, and be moved by it. Where should we be without Milton, Dryden, Pope, Browning, Goethe, Dante — or even Wordsworth?

No motion has she now, no force;
    She neither hears nor sees:
Rolled round in earth's diurnal course,
    With rocks, and stones, and trees.

I still see Eliot's sigh as the sigh of the exile, the prisoner, the refugee, the displaced person, the most typical figures of our murderous, inhumane times. Eliot was speaking of affliction long before Simone Weil taught us to scrutinize the word as if it were a new planet. It haunts all his plays and it was his special burden in the madness of his first wife. And the American Eliot, electing for England, was an exile himself: so too was Auden, going the other way, and from the fashionable, cynical leftism of the thirties into Christianity. I was to make the Christ-wise journey, too, from leftism back to the church of my childhood and to become an exile from the intellectual world of my youth and young manhood, hoping, like Eliot, not to turn again.

> Teach us to care and not to care
> Teach us to sit still.

3

Of course there has been a change in the role of the writer since the twenties, on the eve of which I stood, a boy of thirteen, discovering that what I most wanted to be was a poet. Since then we have created the mass society with the mass media (and the mass deaths too): the radio, the cinema, television, even mass advertising for mass supermarkets. The new media have not only deflected time and attention from literature and journalism, and caused the death of many small reviews, but have somehow 'blocked them off' from the great masses of the population. Everyone thought, in my youth, that a Wells or a Shaw would be as much the spokesman of a mass society as the iconoclast of a bourgeois one. The Wells that I knew certainly saw his role as the great educator and Saul Bellow in *Mr Sammler's Planet* shows what happened to that utopian dream! What the great authors had begun the Worker's Educational Association would complete: or vice versa! It has not happened however (despite the Open University) and no one knows why, though one suspects that the din created by the mass media has a lot to do with it. But the closeness of the writer to the mass media today is a real thing

— every writer at some time finds himself serving them — and a frightening one. He discovers then how colossal is the command of the base and the vulgar, the tripe, over the imagination of the masses, and how little his own standards penetrate. He feels lost in the flood of the third rate and may decide even unconsciously that he can only write, if at all, for his own small circle. Writing becomes a fringe activity rather than a public service.

Some of the fault may lie with the writer. The mass media demand script-writers, copy-writers, producers, serializers, ideas men, adaptors: they offer exciting, absorbing careers: there are even fortunes to be made, and there is certainly more safety. And after all, this is the affluent society in which the writer ought to share, and be valued, in which he is bound to resist the notion that he should be paid or treated as a second-class citizen! This is the feeling behind the demand for the Public Lending Right. Who can quarrel with that? It appears impossible to accept being poor any more.

However, the writer would, I suspect, accept poverty as I did in the twenties and thirties more readily as the price of his freedom than he would today. Then, for very little, a review published here, an occasional poem or short story there, he could get by, ruminating and cultivating his genius in a cottage in the country for seven shillings a week, or room and board at Highgate for thirty-five shillings. I got along for quite a while on a pound or so a week while freelancing. Then, too, when so many were poor, it was an honour to be with them. Today, poverty looks like failure. It is no longer a badge of honour.

That there has been another change in the role of the serious writer in our day no one is going to deny. The difficulty is to establish the sort of change, and which way it is going and whether it is good. Certainly we can see a change from the days of Dickens, when the crowds bought his serials like hot cakes and protested their anguish when the stories did not develop as they wanted — audience participation with a vengeance! — or when Tennyson lorded it over poetry and England like an uncrowned king! Perhaps we shall never get back to that golden age when the writer was at the heart of articulate society, and often its most valid spokesman or most cogent rebel — certainly true of nineteenth-century

Europe. Today there are too many other media of communication and intellectually no longer a unified society. But it was the success of the Victorian writer as the established spokesman (even when in opposition) which still hung like a cloud of glory about the writers who dominated my youth. At least to his age the Victorian writer got through — he communicated, he counted. My gods as a young aspirant to letters were Chesterton, Shaw, Wells, Morris, Richard Jefferies, Aldous Huxley, Siegfried Sassoon, Dreiser and such, and I have to confess, looking back on them, that I still find them truly great. And they, too, seemed mostly to believe in their greatness in a way one seldom finds a writer doing today — and if he did, he would be suspect, immediately! Meanwhile, perhaps through lack of confidence, we have arrived at the idea of a writer as just another technician, albeit with a peculiar trade, yet I think one sees two things in the writer of those days — that he believed in writing as a vocation to which he was called by the muse, or by his genius, or by a sense of mission, or by God, and he knew he was the channel of communication of a fertilizing *something* into the world, and found nothing strange in this, though a modern semantic philosopher would. And then he was ready to accept a prophetic and oracular role over against society, to chasten it, to lash it with scorpions, to denounce it, to inspire it. Can we doubt that is how the great trilogy of the twenties, Shaw, Chesterton, Wells, thought of themselves? We have to look to that brilliant postwar generation in France, to Albert Camus, Jean-Paul Sartre, François Mauriac, or to the contemporary Solzhenitsyn from Russia, to find a close parallel to the England of the twenties as far as the writer is concerned. And that perhaps is because France has not lost the sense of the serious writer as the heart of articulate civilized society, as its moral conscience and prime mover. It is Solzhenitsyn's mission to teach us just that.

I must confess to such a sense of vocation as Solzhenitsyn preaches. I dreamed of being a writer when I was a boy. I conned the tables of literary descent from Chaucer with more eagerness than the tables of dynasties, which I never could remember anyway. I wrote my first short story on the wash stand in my bedroom: it had a hole in the middle where the basin normally went. My story kept tumbling into this emptiness in a Kafka-like manner. It was not a very good story — perhaps it was influenced by the grave into which it kept falling, for every one died, even the narrator in the armchair at his club. But it was in those odd experiences that my sense of vocation was born and sustained by hook or by crook. In lean times and fat ones, I have managed to stick by it, to continue somehow to go on working despite all or against all, even in Army barrack rooms. My aim in writing was never to sell out on what I hoped was my best — intellectually, morally, creatively — though I have not always achieved it. What I thought too, and still think, is that style matters, beauty matters, they count, and that therefore one should not just write, but seek to write with style — for me that is to write with clarity, verve and wit. Writing should reflect and heighten one's joy, one's love of life and people, so that style is not simply a means of intensifying writing, but of intensifying life. Perhaps I may conclude by paraphrasing something that Albert Camus said, that I cannot as a person live without my writing. 'But,' in his words, 'I have never placed my art above everything else. If it is so necessary to me it is, on the contrary, because it separates me from no one else, and enables me to live, such as I am, on the same level as everyone else.' I accept with Camus, that art or writing 'is not a solitary rejoicing' but a means of touching the heart of the greatest number of men by offering them the privileged image of the suffering and joy they have in common.

PART FOUR

*One word of truth is of more weight
than all the rest of the world*
ALEXANDER SOLZHENITSYN

My friend Zelensky, head of Centrosoyus, the Russian Consumer Co-operatives' central organization, party-controlled, had been judicially murdered for putting glass in butter. The Marx brothers had joined the Marxist world. I knew and liked the kindly, worried man. The murder grieved and angered me and made me suspect that Russia had become a land of oriental paranoia, with Stalin as Sultan, rather than the home of socialist planning, and 'workers' fatherland'. Zelensky's cruel death was only one episode in the trail of deaths in the great purges, though he was the only victim I knew personally. Incredibly he gabbled in court:

> I request the Court to permit me to recount the incriminating episodes of my treacherous and criminal activity as a member of the counter-revolutionary traitorous 'bloc of Rights and of Trotskyites', whose aim it was to restore capitalism in the Land of the Soviets.

Then went on to confess to having thrown glass in butter as one step in the process. I knew nothing then of the Gulag Archipelago, but the stench of evil appalled me. I felt in the presence of the witchcraft trials of the seventeenth century in which the victims co-operated with the executioners in their own destruction, with the loathsome Vyshinsky in the role of Matthew Hopkins. If Marxism led to this organized terror, to the destruction of the sons of the revolution in squalid trials, it was necessary to question Marxism relentlessly. But as with my questionings about the spirit, once begun, however reluctantly, where did one end?

I have never been a communist. I was never able to bear the lack of intellectual freedom in the party or all those boring recitals in a barbarous and sterile jargon of a humourless orthodoxy. They repelled me. I was angered too by the party's thorough-going determinism. Marx had in many places taught that a ruling class had power to create and impose a dominant philosophy or culture upon society and that this construct in the world of ideas was the product (and justification) of the prevailing mode of production. The communists I knew, in so far as they thought at all, took this as an iron law, which Marx never did, despite his apothegm that 'determinate individuals . . . enter into determinate social and political relations'. Marx was all for man making and re-making his social and political relations and never explained how these initiatives were possible to one so determinedly determined. No, determinism in Marxism was not only nauseating when mankind was asked to make great decisions, it was also dishonourable: it robbed Marxism of moral responsibility. I had already heard and been stung by Charles Péguy's remark: *'La révolution sociale sera morale ou elle ne sera pas!'* Exactly! It went along with his other great aphorism about the presence of *'capitalistes d'hommes'* in the world. Manipulating the masses, he made me see, might be more dangerous to us all than the manipulation of money bags. Yet all the same, and perhaps because I had a romantic attachment to Trotsky (I took some of his books and pamphlets with me to Russia, as a disinfectant, but the guards threw them out at the frontier), I considered myself, until 1940, an independent, critical Marxist intellectual. I had then almost twenty years of strenuous service to the Labour and Co-operative movements behind me, as leader of a unique working-class youth movement, as editor of more than one left-wing review, as tutor in social subjects to classes of working men and women, as leader of a delegation to the USSR, as a member of Tesarek's cell in the Austrian Social Democratic underground, and of course as writer and poet: a service as varied, as interesting and as committed as it could possibly be, and which, apart from falling in and out of love, was my whole life.

In 1939 and 1940 my Marxism at last began to break under the pressure of world events. I recall at that time reading to a group of young followers in the spring before Dunkirk a long thesis which analysed the Second World War in strictly Marxist terms. As I went on reading my voice faltered. The very language I was using with its endless clichés, 'masses', 'reactionary elements', 'social antagonisms', 'working-class solidarity', 'dialectical materialism', 'the bourgeois powers', no longer seemed to be related to anything real and discernible in the period when Russia and Germany were still at peace and 'the vanguard of the revolution' had contracted by treaty out of the struggle with that which 'was vilest in capitalist reaction'.

Not simply did my mind and my words falter, but the stony silence of my young followers spoke their leaden boredom and dismay. Some were in uniform: the rest were about to be called up. Some were doomed. The political debates of the thirties were now dead to them who had been active in them. Had my argument been faultless it would still have been academic. The world was being torn up outside my window and it was time not only to roll up the maps, but to close the textbooks of nineteenth-century theory. It was my last conscious effort to think in Marxist terms: presently, after surviving the blitz, I too was soldiering.

All my leftism was falling to pieces in my hands. I was trying to fit together a jigsaw of parts which crumbled as I picked them up.

What dusty incoherence it began to look, this museum of 'isms' — materialism, atheism, anti-clericalism, vegetarianism, free-sexism, pacifism, communism, syndicalism, socialism — each with its self-righteous patter, which made up what had been for me the inescapable pattern of leftist thinking and leftist action. Now where was the sense in it all? We had been so sure, and had laughed at the absurdities and contradictions of bourgeois or Christian thought, but to our own we had never confessed. We had raged against the injustices of capitalism — but we believed that justice and injustice were economically determined, that all justice, in fact, was class justice; we argued that man under capitalism was a wage-slave — under socialism we were going to plan everything in the state down to the last shoe-lace; we preached freedom — but freedom, we were convinced, was a bourgeois illusion; we believed that under socialism man's spirit would flower — but we were materialists and did not give tuppence for the spirit; we waxed eloquent about the prostitution of art under capitalism — but as Marxists or Freudians we had no more belief in its independence than in the impartiality of justice; we said war was devilish, we fomented class war.

I acknowledged the original ethical impulse — the generous sympathy with the poor and oppressed — in which leftism was born, but recoiled in sorrow from the malice, envy and social hatreds which were the contemporary fruits of what

111

had begun as a struggle to redeem man from just these things. Leftism now seemed to me to be some kind of disease itself, which I had caught when young, and never been cured of, a disease like that strange condition in which a man loses his sense of balance and crawls and swarms over the earth in the most nauseating contortions when what he most needs is to walk upright. I was sick of leftism, but the world was sick to death, and still is.

Soldiering is a fine way of life if you simply want to think. As I bashed on barrack squares or rushed around yellow gorse commons playing soldiers with my section or dragged my body on long route marches, I asked myself what had gone wrong? What had brought to the ruins of war and political persecution the dream of human perfection?

The force of Marxism derives not just from its analysis of the past, but from its ability to predict. Its basic prediction is (and is still) that the revolution must come from the left — from the proletariat, that is — and is inevitable, and by this history is moved on to its final stage, to the classless society in which the State itself withers away. There was no room in Marxist theorizing for a popular revolution from the right, such as National Socialism turned out to be: still less room for the concept that the revolution of the left and the right could join hands, even if only in expediency, against the rest of the world. Such an act in itself would be counter-revolution. Events inside Russia as well as outside had (for me) come to falsify Marxism and expose its intellectual inadequacy. One had to think again as to the meaning of history and the meaning of man. For the next two or three years of my soldiering, I did so.

The day came when, as a writer, I needed to set it all down. I was by now a Warrant Officer in the Army Educational Corps, lecturing troops in social and military subjects all day long and writing at night in the garret room allotted to me in our Divisional H.Q. What I wrote was published in 1944 by Faber under the title *The Annihilation of Man*. It was subsequently published in America, with appropriate irony, on the day the bomb fell on Hiroshima. Its theme was that the war was symptomatic of, and produced by, a deep and prolonged crisis of the West. The rise of an antihumanistic and antireligious state in Germany and the betrayal by Russia of the

112

humanistic professions of Marxism had their source in the same crisis, I argued. It did not appear an accident that all three major totalitarian regimes (Russia, Germany, Italy) used an apparatus of State terror, standing above the law, against their own peoples. The whole current of liberal, democratic Europe was being turned back, most of all in the most advanced European nation, Germany. The basic error of the ideologies seemed to reside in their view of what man was, and was for. I remember being much helped in this by Peter Drucker's *The End of Economic Man*, which argued eloquently that it was a hopeless falsification of fact to regard man simply as an economic unit (or appetite), that it was socially divisive and led to political disasters: and also by Martin Buber's *I and Thou*, which spoke of the peril of treating men as things. It had long been obvious to me that Marxism's view of man failed to account for his nationalism — that it was inadequate to say the least to describe man purely in terms of his class situation. Historically, his national allegiance was more important. The most powerful political form which had arisen in Europe in recent centuries had been the nation-state, not the class. Indeed, to justify the militancy of his classes, Marx had borrowed for them the historical separation, the sovereignty and right to be above the law which the nation-states had conferred upon themselves. Even the right to war, too.

Yet other doctrines of man were even cruder and more barbaric than Marxist views: worst of all, politically and socially, was the biological-evolutionary view of man that Nietzsche and Spengler had derived from Darwin and Haeckel and advanced with a spell-binding eloquence which had hypnotized Germany. Just as the richness of men's relations with each other and with nature is not exhausted by seizing upon their economic appetites as their *raison d'être*, so the social dynamism of man is not explained by recourse to social-Darwinism, to theories of the morphological evolution of species. The building up of a biological theory into a social mystique is one of the colossal intellectual disasters of our times — it explains not only Hitler but Himmler's earnest and bureaucratic pursuit of the extermination of the Jews in the interest of an evolutionary fantasy of biological race purity. It is sad to see this evolutionary mystique being wished upon

113

Christians and others once again today through the books of Father Teilhard de Chardin, who in a revealing aside said, in *The Phenomenon of Man*, 'monstrous as it is, is not modern totalitarianism really the distortion of something magnificent and thus quite near the truth?'

Teilhard was in the future at the time I wrote *The Annihilation of Man*, though his doctrines were foreseen. In my book I found myself asking something else — not just what had gone wrong with the West's doctrines of man, but also, what did 'gone wrong' mean? Was there a 'correct' doctrine of man against which Nietzschean and Marxist — and possibly Wellsian and Shavian — views could be judged? I was forced to do something which to my agnostic cast of mind was quite unexpected when I began the book — to ask how the ideologies at war around me measured up to the Christian faith, the one central impulse of Europe civilization? It was immediately obvious that both Marxist and Fascist theories of man were inferior to the Christian doctrine in one important respect — they were incapable of universal application. Marxism might be a tenable theory of human progress, but the very condition of its success was that it could offer no salvation, no hope even, to members of other classes. They were expendable. Russians called them, when I myself was there, with uncanny insight, 'former persons'. The bourgeoisie, the aristocracy, the peasantry had to be destroyed as such, if necessary physically, that is, liquidated or murdered. History demanded it. Salvation was the privilege of one class only. Equally, racialist theories, based on a political vulgarization of Darwin's struggle for existance, promised survival or salvation only to those regarded as racially qualified — to healthy Aryans: racially inferior nations could enjoy, as the price of survival, only a role of political subservience not far from slavery: they were to become animals to serve superman.

Christianity, on the other hand, had no meaning historically unless it offered salvation to all men, unless all men of all races, nations, classes, were acceptable to the Lord and equal in his eyes. Of course, this Christian universalism did not of itself make Christianity true, nor was it ever universally applied, but it gave it immense moral prestige. In any case, what had attracted my generation to Marxism was not its exclusiveness, its promise of salvation only to the

114

proletariat, but what we believed to be the universalism of its classless society in which *all* men would be equal. The sufferings of revolution and the 'punishment' of the bourgeoisie (if we thought about them) were only the unavoidable price humanity had to pay for a glorious future. Yet what was revealed by events in Russia was that the application of Marxism in communist hands inaugurated not the loving brotherhood of man but systematic and merciless terror against men, all men, that rule of naked power which Thrasymachus boasted was the only 'justice'.

In contrast, the Marxism of my own generation in Britain was saturated with Christian concepts of the brotherhood of man. It owed much to Sir Thomas More, Robert Owen, William Morris and H. G. Wells. We had imported our own humanity into it, and simply deceived ourselves in assuming that Marxism would get us to our classless Utopia faster than liberal or social democracy. I came to see that the heady vision of a future perfection might be the cause of scorning a present good or even spreading a new evil. The whole notion of a perfected society, Marxist or medieval, the exalted dream which had impelled me for twenty years, began itself to look phoney. It was only an acceptable hope if one argued as Jean-Jacques Rousseau had done, and all my friends automatically did, that man was basically good: when proved not to be good he was corrupted by bad institutions, that was that! Change the institutions and all would be well. At some point early in this internal debate I saw how naive we had been. Man was as capable of great evil as of great good, perhaps more capable, more disposed to it than to good, and would carry this capacity forward into any society or institution we cared to award him, and corrupt it. The Utopian solution, Marxist or Wellsian, was a simple-minded product of politically immature minds which had secularized and brought down to earth the Christian dream of heaven. But of all the idea-systems in vogue in the West (apart perhaps from Freudianism), only Christianity spoke to this deep and grievous human condition, that man is corruptible and self-corrupting and other-corrupting, whatever else he may be. Up to that moment I had been blind to this fact, though the whole world horror had groaned and travailed, since my childhood in the First World War, with the evils of its own creation. More (and today we ought to remember this), it looked in 1940 and 1941 as though European civilization was to be utterly destroyed by its own crimes against men: it seemed to me already evening for the western lands. It was in the shock and anguish of those searing events that *The Annihilation of Man* was written. At the end of the book I found myself doing what I had once thought impossible, defending a Christian view of the world.

It was, and it is worth reasserting it now, when the contrary view is generally held, the sophistication of the Christian doctrine of man which captured me. Only that appeared brave and subtle enough to admit that man was basically good and bad, and capable both of greater evil and of greater good; that with his pride and self-seeking he could soil the finest institutions, and smear with his hatred the noblest gift of the spirit; that he could be redeemed and equally reject his redemption, preferring for himself his chosen evil rather than another's manifest good. The man Christianity spoke about was much more like the man encountered in history, in Shakespeare and Doestoevski and Beethoven, and in the street and the law courts and *The News of the World*, than the pale economic wraith of Marxism or the bloody, strong-toothed animal of Spengler biting his way to superhumanity. Leaving aside the questions I still could not answer for myself about the truth of Christianity, it was plain, but amazing, to me that I was looking at Christianity with warmth and sympathy for giving a valid account of the inescapable human condition. It was a universal diagnosis and prognosis of equal application to Galileans of the first century as to Muscovites of the twentieth. Though the theological terms might sound archaic and unfamiliar they spoke to the truth. It was more easy to understand my world and to have compassion for it once I accepted that man sinned, even against himself, and hated his sin, and sought not only escape from it, but forgiveness and redemption, individually and collectively. And it seemed to me that a religion with so profound a doctrine of man could not itself have arisen from the series of falsehoods I had once held the Gospels to be. At least I conceded they deserved to be examined and reflected upon with the same eager transparency of spirit one brought to great music or poetry or landscape or any other moving experience.

116

One was curious, too. Jesus in his pitifully short life and cruel end had moved so many men so deeply that not simply a world religion but a world-transforming civilization had sprung from the cross. Would he move me? I was circumspect. The supernatural elements of Christianity seemed suspect: about them I was for a while simply agnostic.

2

A few months after that last despairing Marxist paper to my friends I found myself a gunner at Shoeburyness, with one stripe on my arm, employed still in lecturing about social and economic problems in the intervals of standing-to in bunkers along the Thames, waiting for the tardy Germans.

As I walked the Essex lanes, or took the paths across wide, unhedged fields bordered by ragged elms through which came the sea-blink and wave-glitter of the wide estuary, or drove through summer scents of hay and wild briar to my lecturing appointments at gunsites, I wondered what faith was now possible to me. Experiences such as art or poetry, and long-ings for love and for truth, which to materialism were residual, were now to me central to the human condition. They were the guarantee of man's humanity: without them, he would be less than a beast, for he lacked a beast's instinc-tual heritage. And few beasts prey on each other. Man was a creature of the spirit, and witnessed to the spirit, and was nothing without spirit. Could one believe in spirit, and not believe in Spirit, too?

I had been reading a work of Michael Roberts called *The Modern Mind*. It was an effort, on the part of one who had played a part more prominent than mine in aesthetic 'leftism', to say 'good-bye to all that'. Though I do not now remember clearly any particular arguments in it, it fell upon me like a thunderclap as I read it that the way in which my generation wrote and thought was provincial and temporal, peculiar to a certain time and place, even parochial. It was only our arrogance which had made us take it for granted that our way of thinking was the only possible way — the result, like the shape of our bodies, of many centuries of evolutionary

117

struggle to get just where we had got. And that later thinking was superior to earlier thought just because it was later. No such thing, Michael Roberts intimated: this flattering view had to be discarded. It is open to man to *choose* one of *many* valid intellectual positions, many *weltanschauung*, and what I saw most particularly was that man could be equipped with a different set of values from those of my own age: another kind of spiritual geometry would present man with quite another vision of the world. Medieval thought, Dante's or Abelard's, was just such an alternative spiritual geometry, opening up to man's soul visions of heaven and hell closed to the blinkered modern mind. It was not that medievalism was right and modernism wrong: perhaps both were right and both were wrong. The important thing is that they could be different *and* valid. It was possible, without illusion or self-deception to think in quite a different way: 'think', however, is a poor cerebral word for the kind of total apprehension of reality I conceived.

One's total experience, in another climate of time, could add up to a vision, an embrace of reality, foreign to that my contemporaries were making. Man could, like a searchlight beam, swivel himself at the universe. What was in his beam was strangely lit, and sharply true: but this did not mean that there was nothing outside the beam. I felt the beam of my own spirit turning among the stars in an arc which began to embrace the spiritual and personal universe and probe at the cloud behind which might be God.

Nothing of what I am saying really explains the immense tide of hope stirring in me. I saw that I was moving fast to an unknown destination: the rush of my own spirit towards a new freedom was so rapid as to frighten me. I became dizzy at times with expectation of revelation. Walking one night, the thought of the boundless spiritual experience open to man broke suddenly upon me, and I slapped my thigh and said to myself, half-reproachfully, 'You'll be believing in God next!' At that moment I knew that I did, and was at once elated, and afraid of what new obligations this might place upon me. Grace, Péguy said, is insidious: it is full of surprises. One erects a great dyke against it and it trickles through a hairline crack in the base. The struggle to unravel what I did believe moved Christianity from the periphery of my experience to the centre it had occupied in childhood. Christ, the mysterious, suffering figure at the heart of Christianity, the God done to death by man, as man constantly does to death his own spirit, now became, for all one's questions about him, the most moving and frightening symbol in the whole of history. I could see that if it were all quite untrue, that if there had never been a Christ, mankind would spiritually be worse off than if it were historical fact — for that man should have *invented* it, would be the most devastating revelation of the human condition possible, a parable born of the insight of a dark angel into the constant crucifixion of God in the world.

If the world was the scene of a spiritual struggle of which the war against the evil of the Nazi regime was only one aspect, then the decision to exhaust oneself for the victory of the spirit had its origin and resting place in God. With what longing, with what aching of the heart, I sought to come near to this God, and hear his word if he existed and could speak it. But around me there was only the foggy world, closing me in a kind of prison, and the enigma of the men by whom I was surrounded, men like myself, a prey to the same doubts and passions, but into whose inner being I could never hope to penetrate.

Much of this debate with my heart went on while I was lying on my bed in the warm barrack room. But there, the wireless was usually at full blast: an intolerable onslaught on the nerves came from a highly popular programme called 'Penny on the Drum'. When it grew difficult to think I would drift morosely round the room to find someone to play chess with. There was a lance-corporal out of the regimental office who would sometimes play with me, and talk about his wife throughout the game. He would smile wistfully at me when he handled his queen and say, 'I wish it was Jenny. I always try and picture just what she's doing at every moment of the day.' If I had my despair, he had his, and he would live his dreams as he stretched on his bunk in the evening, his eyes filled with tears at the loneliness of his pretty little wife. He had been married only a few months and separation was bitter.

If the barrack room was impossible I would walk, swinging over the ringing road to Great Wakering, to the Exhibition

119

Inn, a vast dome of glittering stars above me, Orion striding high among them, as I had so often seen him about Christchurch spire at home, and the wind coming in from the sea. It was a strange, forgotten coast, reserved and self-communing like all lost lands. Parts of it, even towns along it, like Dunwich, had sunk beneath the waves. The wind perpetually combed it. When the wind was in the west, the grass of the flat, endless marshy islands tossed its manes, the estuary was whipped with grey showers and white horses roamed it. When the wind was in the east the grass lay flat, the estuary was glassy as air, and an invisible, icy, North Sea flood poured everywhere, its blades of cold needling through one's thick rough uniform.

The receding tide left miles and miles of the famous Maplin sands to the sea birds as it went out six, eight, twelve miles in some places. The experimental station on the shore fired its trial shells from ballistic tabernacles along the coast, and measured the invisible flight with their occult instruments. The booming would shake the barrack rooms, and when the driving band of a shell came off it would keen and twang in the air around us like a pursuing spirit. From the tiny shelters on Shoeburyness Front, where the children came to play and talk with me, I would often watch the thin lip of the tide recede until it vanished altogether. And across the barren grey and gold sand the broad-wheeled carts of the experimental station would follow the white rim of water, to dig out the fallen shells which buried themselves deep in the quaking mire, and the carts, too, would dwindle and dwindle until they vanished from sight, clean over the rim of the earth. Here the coast was entirely given up to the flat saltings where the sheep grazed behind ruined dykes, and stranded hulks showed black ribs like the skeletons of whales; the terns hunted prettily, and the peewits played checkers in the sky, and gulls showered down like confetti, while in a score of places the brilliant mallard slept, head under wing, on the shores of those fantastic, grass-crowned islets carved by the sea. No place bare enough to match my own solitude could I have found anywhere else.

One night of great agitation of soul I abandoned the rackety barrack room only to find the sea fog trampling over the garrison town. Often one could watch it slide in from the estuary, a palpable wall riding the tide, and smothering one in the harsh rankness of earth, water and frost. Where could I go? In the schoolroom a class was going on under the rosy gleam of Warrant Officer Meacher, and so I could not sit there and play Schubert's songs on my flute. The NAAFI? The Church Hut? I had little money: I had a wish, too, for quiet and darkness, for the roads in which I heard nothing but my own footsteps sounding frostily on the macadam or echoing from the walls of farm buildings across the black ploughland.

True, the fog was symbolic for me: it was the texture of my own dark turmoil, with its boiling and bubbling. But even a fog is not simply confusion: like a soul it obeys the laws of its being. It was uncanny how one could feel in its motion the turn of a quite invisible tide. In the hour of slack water it would swirl and drift backwards and forwards, an unsteady thing, but let the tide once move in the estuary and it caught the contagion of its motion, and in the inexorable swirl of its fumes past one's freezing ears was a sea rhythm, a measured tread of the waves far away from which it had birth. Sometimes it would flow right out with the retreating tide and leave the air clear and every leaf and twig sparkling with the crystals of its condensation.

By shutting me within myself the fog made the conception which was haunting me as acute as a vision. I wanted to pursue the vision as I walked, but blundering into dripping trees and wet iron gateposts was no joke. It was folly to be slipping blindly about in the narrow Shoeburyness streets, in fear of buses and army vehicles, while my spiritual pulse beat faster and faster. I groped my way into the little cinema and sat, for the very small sum, sixpence or so, which was all I had, on the benches among the leg-swinging, foot-scraping children at the front. The place was airless, with the stale smell of all those shuttered rooms where human beings constantly crowd together. The projector whirred and shot its silver beam through the tobacco smoke, and the vast, inhuman profiles on the screen brayed and bobbed at us. Mothers nursed peevish babies around me, and in the dull bits the boys stamped out to the lavatories. I cannot remember now the films which held the huddled, streaming mass of us silent for most of the time, but the gloaming reminded me of Plato's cave.

121

Let me show you, Socrates said to Glaucon (in the Seventh Book of *The Republic*) how enlightened or unenlightened we really are. Imagine human beings living in an underground den, which has a mouth open towards the light: the creatures of the den have been kept there from childhood, so chained that they cannot turn their heads, but can look only in front of them. Behind them somewhere a fire is blazing and between the fire and the prisoners, files of men are passing and their shadows are projected on to a wall in front of the prisoners. The prisoners would know nothing but shadows and would imagine that the shadows were real. And if they were suddenly released, Socrates asked, and enabled to look at the light, or the sun, or upon real things, would they not be so distressed and dazed as to prefer the dark, and the shadows they understood, to the light which seemed to deceive them? Would they not abuse or kill anyone who tried to teach them otherwise? Are we not, in truth, like these men?

The transcendent reality, now fluttering about my ears, to which I was almost superstitiously afraid to give the word God after all the barren years of denial of him, must, I thought, be rather like the cinema projector: it threw before us the absorbing spectacle of the changing material world. While we had our eyes on that thrilling spectacle it was difficult to doubt its reality, and one forgot to ask by what device it came there. Why ask that of something which was larger than life and somehow more real than one's own heart? But I was now convinced that the world was much like the film — superlatively convincing, and full of the most impressive reality, yet it was in truth secondary and contingent in the universe, it was the projection of the will of whatever lay beyond it, and at one throw of the switch it could be halted and fizzle, as would presently the picture on the screen, into nothingness.

I tried to stare through the screen, and the wall, and the foggy sky beyond, into the very eyes of a God, by whom I myself was seen, holding the universe in the grasp of his hands. 'What a long way I had gone, round and round the houses, only to come back to the most intense conviction, to the first and greatest love of my boyhood and youth.'

3

It was, one might even say, *predictable* that I should find myself posted to the Holy Land. But three years had intervened between the events of Shoeburyness and my arrival in Haifa and these years including writing both *The Annihilation of Man* and *The Living Hedge*. Indeed, Palestine still seems accidental. I was posted to Odessa to take charge of the repatriation of prisoners of war and my posting was changed *en route*. So I found myself, the war in Europe ended, a staff Captain now, lecturing on poetry and politics to troops in the Forces' college on Mount Carmel. I got myself made recreation officer so that I might visit the holy places. Through these circumstances I came to Bethlehem on Christmas Eve, 1945.

Bethlehem is a hill town. It stands out with its belfries, towers and minarets against the sky with a rugged confidence as one comes towards it from Jerusalem. Nazareth had no history until the New Testament story, but Bethlehem was one of the proud centres of Judah, the royal town of David, half fortress and half shrine, on the edge of the Judaean plateau and within walking distance of the wilderness which tumbles down in sandy wastes to the Dead Sea. As the seat of a king and one headquarters of the dominant tribe it was well fitted to be the birthplace of a Messiah. The prophet Micah had declared that the town would bring forth a man of peace who would be the ruler of Israel. Indeed it was because of its importance Jesus came to be born there if the birth story in St Matthew is held to be true. In the census of Augustus, the only way to count people was to gather the tribes together at their natural centres. It does not seem a very reasonable, even practical undertaking, yet for this reason Joseph toiled with Mary from Nazareth, perhaps through hostile Samaria, most probably all the eighty wintry miles from Galilee down the Jordan route to the Dead Sea before climbing up the desert escarpment where the leopards and robbers roamed to the proud little town set on a hill — where so many of the line of David were gathered already that there was no room at the inn for the half-forgotten carpenter and his wife from so far away.

1945 was the first Christmas of peace for seven years and

it seemed as though every soldier in the Middle East had decided to try to get to Bethlehem: some great fervour of hope for our half-destroyed world had gripped us with a hunger we could not conceal. I was on leave in Jerusalem and by the afternoon of Christmas Eve there was already a grumbling flood of military transport of every unlikely kind along the Bethlehem road. It was dark when my truck left under a black sky crackling with stars and frost. But once the town was behind us we forgot the stars for the brilliance of this unusual pilgrimage. After the blackouts of the war one was sensitive to lights — they savoured of the forbidden — and the Bethlehem road was a stream of light in front and behind as vehicles moved along it almost nose to tail. The golden road blazed against the black countryside and when we climbed the hills to the south of Jerusalem we could behold it flowing towards us, one molten unbroken stream. The traffic became slower. Though the military police had planned all this as a military operation, nevertheless block after block halted us as we approached the city. I slipped off the truck and began to walk rapidly to reach the Shepherds' Fields in time for the service. Along the dark rough lanes which lead down past Arab houses to the low-lying plain of Beit Sahur another rivulet of light, this time from hand torches, was dancing like a broad band of fireflies. I had no torch but joined the stumbling press of men. Though men talked and some tried to begin carols, all sounds were blotted out by the mysterious susurration, so heavy and so sad, like a pilgrimage of penance, of so many masculine feet. It was not the sound of an army on the move, for there was no regular beat or tramp, there were no sharp cries of command. We could have been a crocodile of prisoners of war. It was like the night after the ice has broken on an invisible river, and it flows with the scraping, jarring and thrusting of floe against floe, or of ice against its silent embankments.

The night was warm, the houses where Arabs squatted on deep carpets, folding their babies like flowers among them, and eating their evening meal under dim lamps, were open to our gaze: they were another world. On the stone walls Arab boys sat cross-legged, holding out bare hands. 'Johnnee, give, give,' they whispered to us, or just hypnotically, 'Johnnee, Johnnee, Johnnee.' Some marched with us. Presently the glare of a tremendous bonfire lit our faces. Drifts of singing came up. The service had started and this lent fuel to our impatience. It took an interminable time to reach the fire in that excited throng of men, but round its crackling the press was so great that there was almost nothing but the flames to be seen or heard. I joined in the carols as soon as I knew what was being sung. After a while I grew anxious about the time for I wanted to be in the church on the square at midnight and on these occasions a panic overcomes me. I am one of those who is always sure he will never be in the right place at the right time. In any case I could not get anywhere near the blazing heart of the service in the Fields but drifted around the smoky circumference. Presently the flood, I in the vanguard, began to return, scuffling the stony lanes, to the great square before the Church of the Nativity where thousands waited for the midnight bells which would proclaim again the Birth. The streets and alleys round the church were like a medieval fairground. The yellow lights tawnily striped the canyon walls of houses. Acetylene flares made the monastery walls flicker with a pantomime unreality. A cloud of smoke and dust rose in the air, luminous with the town lights. Stalls were piled high with oranges, with brilliant green and yellow sweets, with flat bread, with bread in crisp golden bangles, with nuts roasting on charcoal fires red as poppy petals, with freshly baked cakes and great glass flagons of coffee and lemonade, shining like lamps. Hawkers and cheap-jacks pestered the soldiers. The coffee sellers clanged their brass cups. The beggar girls and prostitutes had left Jerusalem streets to ply their trade here. Everywhere Arab children swarmed — stealing, fighting, quarrelling and begging cigarettes or money, bullying the warmhearted African soldiers who are never able to resist the appeals of children, and who laugh and laugh as lovingly they give in.

The Church of the Nativity has only one door on its Crusader front — made deliberately small so that horsemen should never ride in to massacre. Through this portal we slowly crushed our way. There was no hope of reaching the Franciscan chapel, let alone the crib below where only a few can ever gather at a time before the altar beneath which, tradition says, Jesus was born. The beadle stamping his steel-tipped staff of office had difficulty in making a way for the crocodile of olive-skinned choirboys in red surplices and lace cottas which hand in hand and with decorous excitement was snaking its way through the waiting crowd. I came out again, though with difficulty, through incense clouds, to hear the bells and to be silent under the sky. As the hour approached everything became quieter. One could now hear from somewhere in the church the processional psalm of the Franciscans. Sitting exhausted on the low wall around the square of the Nativity, free at last of children, were African troops, some of whom I knew had been here all day, perhaps without food. They were immobile and expressionless lolling there, waiting for the bells. The square became more packed. A hush of expectation passed over us. In the silence it was painful to breathe. The slack negro soldiers gathered their loose limbs together and with faces agape stood up slowly, caps in hands. The chimes the world has heard so many times on the radio came over the square. A waiting group started a carol. Christmas Day had come to the seat of the nativity. With relief and joy I walked slowly to the Lutheran church where the Anglicans were singing the first eucharist of Christmas Day.

4

Some years later I returned to the Holy Land — no longer Palestine, but divided between Arabs and Jews of course — and stayed with the nuns on the Mount of Beatitudes on Lake Galilee with an Israeli gunpost under my window and Syrian infiltrators in the lost fields between our nunnery and the Jordan entry into the lake. I used to go down to Capernaum almost every day. Here is one diary entry I made which throws light on my pursuit of that inner vision which is the subject of this book.

Over Galilee there is not a cloud to ascend into today. The lake is purest sapphire, a jewel in the Lord's ring. Every distance is so sharp that I can see the eagles over Tiberias rock. This is how I remember Galilee in 1945, a world cut by a gemlike light and a wind like music. The sky is mild and the air is soft: the khamsin has blown itself out.

I walked to Capernaum through the banana groves, past the Bedouin camp. The dogs which were silent and sleeping suddenly woke when I was among the tents and surrounded me bristling, grinding bare teeth. Their hair stands right on end, which frightens me more than their barking. They were called off. The principal Bedouin tent has an enormous shiny wireless cabinet standing in it. Real? Show? Driven by a battery — many batteries? Concealing a cocktail bar? I never hear it playing.

At Capernaum I am always greeted by the frail, dove-eyed young Franciscan who lives in the great, grim manse and acts as custodian. His gentle eyes light up as he sees me and he comes loping after me through the rows of basalt querns and millstones arranged in a kind of open air museum and takes me by the arm, hailing me in his staccato French. It is so quickfire that I can't grasp everything he says, though I do my best to make a conversation. He pulls me round and places hands on my shoulders and stares at me pleadingly. We must pray for unity, he says. It is a grievous thing (*chose méchante*) that the church is divided. Do I not agree? Are we not all for Christ, and all in Christ? Not just his large dark eyes, but his whole body is full of spiritual pain. Almost daily he receives parties of tourists of every denomination and of none. Their reverence, their happiness have deeply affected him. He cannot bear the thought of our formal Christian divisions: it becomes more and more a cross he must bear. (*C'est vrai, ce que je dis?*) His suffering is so great that tears come into his eyes. If he could stretch out there in the shade of the synagogue and die so that the whole church was reunited, he would do so, at this very moment! *J'offre à Dieu ma vie seule pour l'unité Chrétienne.* I comfort him as best I can, or we comfort each other, but the words are thin, dry, things compared with the fact of division before which we are both helpless and downcast.

The synagogue has become for me a place of prayer and I had it to myself today, after the young unhappy Franciscan had left. I brooded and meditated alone by the colonnade watching the light play among the gale-blown eucalyptus which make a poem of the place, fingering the

127

worn, hot stone, its rough grain and millennial endurance, and seeking understanding in the warm smell of seeding herb and the sun-distilled essence of aromatic blue gums and the iron and water smell from the lake. I prayed with all the intensity of which I was capable, as ready to cast myself down as the Franciscan had been. If only by some prayer intensity I could reach the heart of the place I believed I might live the illumination of its history too. I have only a few little prayers about myself, only one of which concerns my writing. I prayed it first when I went to Walsingham on pilgrimage to ask for the opportunity to write the books I was engaged upon. It asks for 'the grace, the means, the readers, the courage, the truth, the life'. This day I prayed this, but prayed myself beyond it into a tense silence, but a silence which asked for a sign. A sign! In a stillness in which only the sun rang and which stretched my soul almost to breaking I reached the point where I believed that the Lord might appear and heard (my hands were over my face) a swooping, rushing and rustling before me which made my spine tingle. I could hardly move. When I removed my hands I saw, to my discomfiture, the Franciscan's ginger dog rolling in the dust before me and smirking. His whisking tail had created the sounds of flight. When he caught my astonished stare he leapt up to fawn upon me and lick me and kept me company for the rest of my meditation. The soul life prayer was not lost: it went on among the honey and the blue and basalt stones and tall rife tansy — 'the light, the light, the seeking, the searching, in chaos, in chaos'.

My first visit to Caesarea was in an army truck in wartime. It was even then a decayed, neglected corner of Palestine. We swung off the main coastal road towards the sea along pot-holed lanes quick with the sand of dunes which are the only true land here. Boulders had been dropped into holes to make the roads passable to army vehicles. We raised swirling silvery genies as we ricochetted along with as much care for our springs and our limbs as we could contrive. We passed a few poor, beautiful and insanitary Arab villages and then came to an area where the earth was brown-grey and littered with rubble. The sand had gone. The land was suddenly reminiscent of a cleared bomb site. The small stones might have been shattered bricks. The Arabs scratched at the stony place: they piled the stones in neat heaps in corners of their fields and erected low unmortared rubble walls to divide their patches or to control irrigation. They had ploughed and scratched for centuries but still the stones came for they were ploughing across the rubble of a city. Seaward at one point the land ended in sheer cliff, fifteen to twenty feet high, a cliff of rubble. Within the rubble dunes of the Herodian city we found the remnants of the Crusader city, within that again the poor Turkish town. To seaward rows of blackened Roman columns washed in the surf.

It was important, my friends said, not only to see the Crusader and Herodian remains of this once great city, but to meet George, a brigand in a slouch hat and khaki denims with a fast line in patter. George was a Greek Orthodox character, verger of the Greek chapel in the village to which once in a blue moon a proper priest came along to hold a service. They were afraid that George might not last very much longer because recently there had been an affray between Moslems and Christians in which a Greek priest had been killed. They were attached to George if only for his pure villainy and thought that for some of the British officers to call might strengthen his morale.

We went to his house. Was he really living over the apse of some Crusader chapel? I hesitate to say this now for it seems so improbable. To reach his house one opened a ramshackle little wicker gate of the kind one sees in country gardens. A weight attached to a chain makes sure it slams shut after one has passed through: this saves the chickens from straying. George had just such a crazy gate, but the weight which operated it was the mutilated torso of a Roman cupid. His chickens were housed in huts made of driftwood and petrol tins lifted high off the ground by fragments of marble frieze to protect them from rats. It was the same everywhere. A flight of steps, rounded and gothic and majestic, mounted to a miserable Arab backdoor. A Moorish arch was tied by a strip of marble Roman carving. The Crusaders had borrowed chunks of Roman marble and black and red granite pillars to bind their masonry. Pigs stabled in an ancient crypt fed from troughs which once were the elegant baths of Roman ladies, and the blind marble face of an emperor stopped a hole in the roof.

George offered us cups of muddy Turkish coffee and pieces of fly-haunted melon and sought to persuade us to buy an Arab dancing girl's head-dress which he said had belonged to a Roman slave and we could have for two pounds. He took us to a room where, to my fancy, our army boots slurred over Crusader vaults beneath and tried to sell us coins, medallions and other tourist trifles, and when we proved resistant to his sales appeal routed his naked four-year-old son out of bed and sent him round, his liquid eyes mechanically pathetic, to fawn and beg 'piastre' from us. The child had the perfect domed head, small chin and almond eyes of the Byzantine respresentations of the Infant Jesus.

We cut the hospitality short and began a tour of the village. We were shown Salome's pool where, George said, women bathe if they are barren, and the place where St Paul was chained to the rock — only the rock was not there; a priest, he said, had removed it. We clambered into Crusader remains and over the Byzantine walls, probing among the shards and ruins of the crumbling Herodian terraces by the sea, always in the hope that a casual kick would dislodge something which one could take away in one's pocket. The ruins of the great moles stretched out to embrace the Mediterranean and between them, in surf more brilliant and rushing than in the desert one had remembered, rolled the rows of marble and granite columns which had once made Caesarea the Rome of the Palestine coast. No other worthy trace of this glory then remained. The dusty little Arab village, with its down-at-heel café where the local inhabitants sat and played checkers on stools which ought to have collapsed before the First World War, crouched between the battered walls and the stunted minaret by the entrance to the quay. Babies and dogs and flies swarmed in the dust. It was as poor and as lost and as hopeless as an eastern village could be, without a glimmering even of the tourist value of its once ancient glory. Only George, the self-appointed dragoman of the town, saw its possibilities. And George took us to the mosque. At the sight of it I was prepared to forgive this baking little town its sleazy horror. It was a lofty whitewashed room, Crusader simplicity and strength itself, with the plainest of rose-red rugs on the floor. Tombs of saints stood in one corner, and in the other the white prayer niche, the simple pulpit. The mosque stood on the old quayside. It was lit by one tall, shining window of plain glass wide open to every trembling run of light from the breaking sea beneath. It had the elemental quality of purity and simplicity possessed by a tent in the desert or a white-sailed ship at sea, and I was too moved to speak.

On a much later visit after the partition, with John Ryecart (priest at St Luke's, Haifa), his wife and small son, I found a totally deserted city of interest only to archaeologists. George and his family had gone. The Arabs had vanished. Broken shutters slammed in the perpetual south wind which had caused the city to be built. Sand ran in rivers along the empty streets and piled unswept against northern walls. There was not a pane of glass, a piece of furniture, a chicken, a mangy dog anywhere. I could not even find the apse on which George's house had once rested. Through the rooms and arches and over the ruined quays of this ghost village resting on many ghost towns, it was possible to scramble as one had done before in the hope of dislodging a relic or tile or a coin. But with still more sadness than in the past. I did find again the miraculous little mosque which once reflected on its windows and its ceiling the thrashing surf, the beauty of which had haunted me for a decade. It was smashed. The great window on the sea had gone: the whitewash was peeling from the walls. The tombs of the saints had been battered open by hammers and used as latrines, the walls had been daubed with slogans and threats and over the simple door with its inscription to the glory of Allah, someone had painted a skull and crossbones in red and added in Hebrew the inscription, 'Death to the Arabs'.

How does one speak of these experiences? The friendly dog at Capernaum seems now like an ironic commentary on my effort to command God. All the same, what peace there was among those old stones under the rifle sights of the Syrian sharpshooters! I had rather been there under fire than in Caesarea. And what sadness in the gentle Franciscan. But that other, that pure white cell running with the reflections of the blue and white murmuring sea, with its gentle old men reciting the Koran in the face of that beauty, how could it become so lost, so defiled, so beshitted? It was a blow to the heart, a stroke against God. One could understand Berdyaev, that it was not a natural thing but a spiritual thing for men to love one another. The natural thing was for men to hate and kill each other.

5

When I left the Army I settled down at Battersea in a flat in a block of mansions overlooking the Park, and put my name on the electoral role of All Saints, the church at the corner, a decaying red brick building grimed with London's smoke even though barely a century old. (It has burnt down since.) I was for a time about the only man in the congregation, or so it seemed to me when the harassed and overworked priest, who had borne the weight of the years of severe raids particularly there close to Victoria and the power station, preached at men in the parish for their failure to give a hand. When I asked how I might help, I was told I could serve, if I knew how and had a mind to. I relished the irony: serving at the altar was the last task I had done for the church when, in my teens, I had abandoned it. It seemed I had to begin again where I had left off and for this I retrained myself: I was to go on serving or helping in some similar capacity at the church for fifteen years, about the longest post-war spell in any one place. The role of an acolyte or server in a Church of England Mass is to light candles, or carry a candle, or the cross, move the missal as the service requires from the epistle to the gospel side of the altar, present the priest with the elements, bread, wine and water, at the appropriate moment, and assist in the ritual ablutions. He plays a part in that beauty and order which I described in an early autobiography as a holy dance before the Lord. There comes a moment when he is in the way — when the congregation comes to the altar rail to receive communion. Different churches have different procedures for making him inconspicuous. At All Saints we knelt painfully on the sanctuary floor tiles or on the altar carpet's edge, almost at the reredos, and in prayer. Fierce and intense prayer was necessary for me if I were to reach oblivion of my aching kneecaps and it became a moment in my weekly life when it was possible to melt the ego away and to submit imploringly to God. One saw the point of the exercises followed under pain and discomfort in monasteries. The pain gave one a hard and realistic knowledge of one's tyrannical body: it disallowed the drift into an amiable godly daydream: it did not rule out but somehow made possible the suspension of the ego and the opening of the self to God who at that solemn moment in the Mass might cross over those vast distances of infinity and come to man of his own choosing. I knew (or thought I knew: it seemed so much to hope for) when God had been: it was not only that the pain went but that words ceased and a light of a peculiar texture and fragrance spread through one's being. There came an Easter, a particularly happy Easter for me, when my timorous belief about these visitations became certain knowledge. The Anglican Easter morning service is a beautiful one: in lilies white and gold and vestments white and gold the Church hails the festival day: no one, however poor his faith, could fail to be moved by the adoration of the risen Christ: but the tally of communicants that Easter Day was a long one, and the priest single-handed. We were not yet at the days when a layman could assist. I was lost in my prayer at the north end of the altar when the gold flame filled me with its warmth and brightened to white and I lost all consciousness of where I was and what I was doing. Time was suspended and there was no world either. When I woke from this trance-like suspension of being in the awaited Christ the service had finished with its communicants and was moving on to the Gloria. Something in my kneeling attitude perhaps had persuaded the priest to leave me undisturbed in my private place.

The visit seemed a pure and undeserved gift for which I dared not *ask* again, but might wait in simplicity for whatever might befall. I had no wish to begin special disciplines or mystical exercises through which the experience might be repeated. I was too afraid of self-deception — that I might persuade myself that such things had happened out of a euphoria which had other causes. Perhaps in this I was wrong and the disciplined mystic will rebuke me for a failure of nerve. I would accept the rebuke and say only that I was filled through and through not only with consciousness of the presence of God, but with the belief that he could not be commanded.

PART FIVE

And death shall have no dominion
DYLAN THOMAS

1

My oblique and hesitant return to Christianity did not solve my intellectual and moral problems. Or rather it solved some, only to open others as formidable. Was Christianity, in essence, true? This was a far different question from, for instance, what was the social and cultural impact of Christianity, which was also crucial. Then, as difficult, who was Jesus and what was his nature? I have been squaring-up to these questions since the Second World War. Even during that war I was, in the Middle East, reading and making notes for the book that was ultimately published as *The Meaning of Human Existence*. But I offer here only some meditations on the life of Jesus and its significance for us as pressed upon me by all that had happened to me religiously.

When I asked myself, even as a boy, 'Do I, can I, believe in God?', Jesus was an irrelevancy. I cannot recall any of my friends ever saying, 'I don't believe in Jesus,' though monotonously they said, 'I don't believe in God.' In due course I read the literary detective stories which disposed of the existence of Jesus, or turned him into the principal of a religious drama, or explained the resurrection as the product of a conspiracy. I surrendered myself to *Brook Kerith* by George Moore, vivid with the poetry of Galilee, which allows a recovered Jesus to become an exile in an Essene monastery in the desert where an incredulous Paul chances on him, and not long ago I read the most recent of the conspiratorial reconstructions, Hugh Schonfield's *The Passover Plot*, at once well informed and preposterous. All that sort of thing led Gilbert Chesterton, who became a friend, once to say, 'Of course, Jesus Christ never existed, it was another man, *called* Jesus Christ.'

My trinitarianism was always faulty: it still is. The *son* of God was never quite the same thing as God to me. He was an offshoot, the junior partner: as Eusebius writes, 'secondary' to God, 'and ministering to his Father's commands'. One's atheism turned upon the existence of God: one did not have to doubt that Jesus had lived. The intolerable question as to whether Jesus was God was secondary to God's existence. If one did not believe in God, the question was answered. A good man, one said, but deluded, and executed as a religious and political rebel. Divinity was something his followers had thrust upon him.

If one believed theistically in God, as I did passionately as a boy, then Jesus was validated. God, erect over this universe, lent credibility to Jesus, and urgency to his message. It was then possible to accept him as the Son, actually or symbolically, and to believe that he himself knew or found his role. His mission made grieving sense. Take away the Almighty and Jesus thirsts in the barren desert with the rest of us. To this position I still adhere.

It is the opposite of many contemporary theological trends. They say — concentrate upon Jesus, he is all we know. If we are to understand anything of God, by definition unknowable, it is only by saturating ourselves in the life and passion of Jesus. Jesus is God's paradigm. There in him is God made plain, and nowhere else, and you must live with this painful limitation. Or, like *The Secular Meaning of the Gospel*, by Paul T. Van Buren, they say there is only Jesus — no God, no transcendence, no divine dimension, only 'the Man for others'. Yet, leaving aside the ambiguities attributed to Jesus (for example, in John 14: 'Anyone who has seen me has seen the Father,' 'no one comes to the Father except by me,') if the critics will allow us, Jesus never seeks to establish a monopoly of worship or of authority. 'Why call me good? Only God is good.' He appears to act always under God and seeks only to serve the will of God. 'He who loves me will be loved by my Father.' 'Yet not my will but thine be done,' at Gethsemane and his reproach to God for forsaking him, witness even on the cross to this too. Jesus comes to his mission through baptism by John, like an ordinary God-fearing man, in a nation more God-centred, more God-consecrated, than any which has ever existed. Life for a Jew was fearful with the majesty and judgement of God. No one could have preached either religion or morals or agitated politically in Israel without being securely anchored in the Godhead. It was not possible for Jesus to conceive himself a solitary demi-God. God validated him and he suffered, praying with sweat and tears for that validation. The attribution of divinity to Jesus was not a way of isolating him from

138

a previous theistic tradition, but of entrenching him more firmly within it. No, the modern theological, christological effort to bet all upon the life and passion of Jesus is an effort to save Christianity in the face of the contemporary inability to speak about God at all. It is an act of despair. So let me say again, for the boy I was, it was obligatory to begin with God not Jesus as the key to my atheism.

Besides, I pitied Jesus. Dared one pity God? As a school-boy who loved green hills I could not escape the fact that on one of them 'The dear Lord was crucified, who died to save us all.' *God* crucified? By *men*? Was it possible? Necessary? In a confused form it burned with me but there was no one to whom I could blurt out the questions. I saw that men could hate Jesus for the goodness he was asking of them — turning the other cheek, giving up one's cloak, forgiving seventy times seven, forsaking riches — or for the savage attacks he made on his generation of vipers, and that they would want to kill him for his infuriating persistence. One had met this anger when trying to dissuade other boys from some entertaining piece of badness. All that was comprehensible. But what had Jesus, or God, got out of it? Nothing, it seemed, except defeat. There he was, the vanquished Son, dying in agony on the cross and no more able than other men to assuage his bitterness. 'He saved others: now let him save himself.' The jibe bit deep. It was another instance for me of that sad 'I told you so' my halfpenny history book had taught me. The angels, the shepherds, the star-drawn Kings at Bethlehem were the glory, yes, but be patient, turn the pages and learn how you were to be fooled.

2

I suppose I must have heard the words 'redemption' and 'atonement' in my youth. They made no hard impact, but sacrifice I understood. 'Greater love hath no man than this, that a man lay down his life for his friends' cut to my heart's core. I courted such a sacrifice, and when I learnt how David risked his life to face Goliath or some soldier stayed at his post till he died to protect his comrades, all my being applauded. I regretted only that my opportunity had not come. Jesus was said to have died to save us *all*, and so his was the perfect sacrifice. Yet how was this true, I longed to know? What were the dangers men were safe from after the crucifixion which they had not escaped before? I could not frame my question so succinctly then, but the confusion and sorrow in my mind was born of my feeling about it. Why did Jesus, of all men, have to die in this cruel way? Why did God so savagely require it, and what did he hope to gain from it? He died for our sins, the Prayer Book said. He was 'the propitiation for our sins'. I cannot believe that either doctrine, if explained to me then, would have pleased me.

Propitiation was an act to avert someone's anger, the sacrifice of something precious to a superior power, as Abraham prepared to sacrifice his son, but was prevented by God. But God did not intervene to save his own, infinitely dearer Son. Then *who* was being propitiated — God the Father? God the Father's wrath against sinners was actually being stayed by the sacrifice to himself of his own Son? Oh monstrous, monstrous! If the propitiation was not addressed to omnipotent God, then to whom, to what? To the fates? There was in all primitive religion, as in Greek drama, the sense that one's life or the lives of one's loved ones might be overtaken, destroyed, by dark unknown forces even then preparing to move unseen. The propitiatory acts were acts of fear. How, possibly, could fear motivate Jesus? He seemed so fearless for himself. That he was fearful for us made more sense. But how would propitiation help us?

I could see that the contemporaries of Jesus might be saved by his act. Like the scapegoat driven into the wilderness he bore the burden of their sins upon his back. One can see him saying 'Father, accept my life for their redemption — take me, not them,' — making his voluntary sacrifice as an examplar to all men of how far *his* love for them went: yet his love was not the same as the Father's love, if that existed. Yet Jesus died for our sins too, before we were ever born to commit them and so it seemed that mankind was not spared from sin after all, despite the death upon the cross. Although the shadow of Golgotha has been over every generation since, and blackest upon those who called themselves Christian, men went on sinning. Of what use was it all then? The sacrifice was made to seem derisory.

The circumstances of the Passion injured (for me) the overflowing love that Jesus taught that he and the Father bore for their children. I am not thinking of the manifest failure of God to do for Jesus what he had done for Isaac, which troubled me as a youngster, but of the punitive apparatus Christianity proceeded to erect against sinners — who were not only those who did evil but those who rejected Christ — consigning them to the torments of hell. There were still hellfire preachers around in my childhood and they were deeply disturbing. One met them more often in chapel than in the placid and decorous Church of England. For them, it was clear that God saw all, and one was going to be judged. For an act of propitiation to have meaning there had to be a terrible but accessible judge who could be moved by it, and sinners who could be spared the rod. The theology of eternal reward and punishment asserted that not all sinners were going to be saved. Who were the sinners? Roughly all mankind of course. Some Calvinistic preachers said only a foreordained elect would be saved and enjoy heavenly bliss: and they were only preaching in tune with the Thirty-nine Articles of Religion of the Church of England. For the rest God and Dante knew what was in store for them. But love? *Love*?

A precocious fifteen, I wrote, in a penny red Lion exercise book I bought to put down my meditations, a study of sin. I said, never having heard of Pelagius, that man was as God had created him and if that included the power to sin man was no more responsible for that than for his blue or his brown eyes. If man was to overcome sin then he had to be given the power to do that by God, too, and was no more to be praised for his goodness than blamed for his badness. *Q.E.D.*

Nevertheless, I could not express my hard, real difficulties about my Christian faith as clearly then as now. I was baffled by the role and the meaning of Jesus in the religious life. The questions about him came so thick and fast. The matter could not be bottomed. It was easier to live with the notion of a supreme God, the Creator, who had not got himself soiled in the mud of our lives, who represented for me the joy and the serenity of a universe which fired me with delight every day. When in manhood I made my long and circuitous return to the faith, Jesus was the absent member of the

141

Trinity. Perhaps I had replaced him with 'man'? For it was man who concerned me, a serving soldier, lecturing to troops daily about war and the causes of war, the rise of National Socialism, the Russian Revolution, the future of the West, the rights of man, and so on and on. I was haunted not just by the events we were living through but by the tragedy of the human situation.

Writing of the formation of his ideas (those that underlie *Lord of the Flies*) William Golding made a fearful indictment, 'Man distils evil as a bee distils honey.' In the same historical context as Golding I had discovered evil again. But evil on such a scale against man and God, hurling men, women and children into such abysms of suffering, that the world's destroyers and the world's destroyed were both dehumanized. It could barely be held in the trembling mind. And I thought — we do not even begin to understand man in all his nihilistic complexity. We have invented a man to believe in because we found the truly inhuman man too much of a monster to contemplate. But now that the mask has worn thin and we find only the headpiece filled with straw, our bad faith over ourselves is exposed. Luther said that man hated God, he had a passion against the deity, Berdyaev said that man did not want to be human, only God wanted man to be human, but man resisted this to the utmost. Both might have said that man hated his own species.

It was this rent through the human spirit, man at war with man and with God, sometimes with the best intentions, that I tried to expose in *The Annihilation of Man*, writing it in the cold badly-lit barrack rooms or on tea-puddled NAAFI tables.

Yet the discovery of man's inhumanity through a close look at the battle of the ideologies is inadequate as an explanation of what was driving me towards Christianity. Indeed by speaking of the historical forces at work in the West one evaded the other side of the question, the quality of one's personal life. I remember the shock that came to me when I read that John Stuart Mill asked himself whether he would be any happier or better or more worthy if all the reforms for which he had so eagerly campaigned were accomplished? He had to answer, no. I saw that was true for me too and recognized that fighting for social causes could be a surrogate for personal unhappiness, a way of evading the truth about oneself. (But not fighting could be an evasion too.) I had thrown myself with immense vitality and idealism into building up a youth movement and when that was accomplished found myself poor and ill and futureless and without job or hope, no more able to see how I was to go on than H.G. Wells's hero in *The Dream*.

Poor H.G. Wells! In *The Dream* he tried to show us the painful difference between the life of miserable little Henry Mortimer Smith round about Folkestone in the period of the First World War and his reincarnation in Sarnac, the noble Utopian, in a rustic Utopia William Morris could have invented for the year 3000. Wells was wholly on the side of Sarnac. But Smith, not Sarnac, takes over the book. One cannot believe in Sarnac but one identifies immediately with Henry Mortimer Smith. It is the comic and bitter realism of his frustrated lower middle-class life with its struggles, jealousies and dishonour which dominates the book. And Wells's defeated little men whose capacities fall so far short of their idealistic strivings spoke for us all. We too assumed public lives of honour and nobility and lived inner lives of calculated bad faith. Politics for instance taught one to lie with enthusiasm, with a generous open face, to feel rewarded by the smiles of happy acceptance of the lie in the audience, even by the demand for it there, to feel clothed by mendacious saintliness. There is nothing so exalting as the common, the mass proclamation of a lie: one bursts with pride at having sold it so successfully. So the humbug of one's own life was a special challenge. Once one had come to recognize it one could not go on living by it. There had to be a search for honesty. On the processes of politics and economics one could have some effect, of course. It was a necessary part of one's citizenship. But about the inner integrity of one's own life one could do much more. The more and more one lived a purely external — extrovert — life devoted to causes, to business, to sport, to getting on or keeping up the easier it was, as Charles Darwin found, for the inner life to atrophy, deprived of water, of sun, of discipline. Indeed it could go so far, as I saw in the lives of my friends and colleagues, that the spirit seemed to cease to exist. Yet without the soul everything is meaningless. One might as well be reincarnated into a railway time table. One had become a hollow man with

143

a dried voice like rats' feet over broken glass.

3

The spirituality I sought to hold to when I began my return to Christianity was the God-man dialogue which Martin Buber so brilliantly expounded and for me, as for him, as our talks together brought out, the life of the spirit was that world between man and God which the dialogue created. We usually think of the totality of human culture as a kind of discourse between men and nations and civilizations across space and through time, so that Socrates speaks to Confucius, Newton to Einstein, Kant to Bertrand Russell, Homer to Goethe and Phidias to Henry Moore. Perhaps nowhere is this man-to-man dialogue more obvious than in music. Yet I began to see the totality of this cultural life, in which man was most truly man, as also the dimension in which man co-habited and co-created with God. *Also?* No, *primarily.* God was the mysterious third partner in the arena in which man wrestles, bruised, with his destiny like Jacob with his angel and seeks to shape it or falls back exhausted from the task.

Yet Christianity is not, in so many words, about so rare-fied a theme. It is more brutal and direct and uncompromising. It was not in origin a dialogue such as we might have had from Plato. It was not even a Christian discourse such as came from Aquinas or Augustine. It was pretty incoherent. Even the words of Jesus in the Gospels come across as a jig-saw puzzle still. The letters, the records, the explanatory discourses came after the painful events, and the events were a young human life which ended in tragedy. That was plain, whatever subsequent interpretation one placed upon that life. The drama of this life was everywhere imprinted on the West, the parables and sayings of Jesus were woven into the folk life and language; the betrayal and the crucifixion, and the lessons drawn from them, were to the yearly religious cycle as though they had happened that year.

A sailor on board ship, according to a medieval story, picked up a Jewish passenger on a Good Friday and threw him overboard. 'Why did you do that?' screamed the Jew, in danger of drowning. The sailor shook his fist at him. 'You crucified our Lord,' he shouted. The liturgy hammered home this immediacy; the sacrifice of the Mass underlined it. Jesus was forever being crucified afresh. He became a symbol spread across the heavens of human suffering and human perfidy to God. This was the figure I faced in vast unease as Christianity drew me. And it was to his challenge that I had sooner or later to make reply and did not do so until I attempted a biography of Jesus, a thing I was told you should not do. Of course one should not; the materials for a biography are not there. The Gospels are *aide-mémoires* with a liturgical rather than a biographical significance: we have been told this *ad nauseam* by the theologians and form critics. Nevertheless Jesus had a life or he had nothing. He was not just a lay figure operated by a priesthood, and it would be strange if nothing of the quality and even of the detail of that life seeped through, despite editorial distortions and slantings. And however we label the Gospels, niggling over the semantics, the precise purpose of the Gospels in the churches for over two thousand years has been to display the life and passion and teaching of Jesus to the faithful as a succession of real events and not just as religious symbols or moral examples. There are times when it is better not to play safe but rather to risk the disapproval of the theologians in order to make that life real to me and to others who might have the same difficulties. One problem is that of the *unreality* of Jesus in his ecclesiastical setting. Perhaps one is simply speaking of over-exposure, over-sell. The omnipresence of the image of Jesus in Christian culture, the endless repetition of the Gospel stories, the crucified man of Christian art, must have been subject to the law of diminishing returns. One cannot endlessly grieve, endlessly mourn. The Christ-figure becomes blander, simplified almost to caricature, fused into an accepted background to which one pays less and less conscious attention. Even the terrible death becomes a stylized act, handled without emotion, for of course this death is what has to happen to the Christian God-man, it is fore-ordained and accepted by Jesus and the Father as redemptive for us, it has to recur every Easter, we are attuned to it, so what is asked of us is no more than a ritual show of grief. Our guilt is diminished and if we wake in the night we

145

need not suffer anguish but turn over again into our smooth moral sleep, Golgotha forgotten.

Greek statues were originally painted, which must have heightened their human impact. The centuries have eroded the colour and we are left with the enjoyment of the pure form where the Greeks, facing Laocoon and his sons wrestling with the serpent, were shocked as we might be by a photograph or film of a catastrophe. Some such draining of reality from the Gospel story has taken place. People speak derisively of the stained glass image of Jesus as though the Church had deliberately corrupted his image. One cannot believe this was ever intended. The Church, was, rather, the victim of its earnestness in keeping the image of Jesus before the eyes of man. It was its central task, the reason for its existence, and it was more than successful. But it is also a self-falsifying process, subject to the legend-building that goes along with the memorials of half-mythical heroes, such as our own Arthur of Britain. One cannot imagine what would have happened to the legend of Jesus had there been *no* documents coming down from his time from his own friends and disciples, men he loved and who died for him. This is historically remarkable too.

Our time has witnessed an enormous expansion of higher criticism. The New Testament has long been the quarry of a textual mining industry, the results of which are hardly even a rumour to the man in the pew. The final result has been the process of demythologizing associated with the learned Bultmann: the story of Jesus, the hypothesis goes, was retailed in the language and concepts of the first century which make doutful sense in ours. It is in those terms only that we learn of him. Jesus ascends into heaven, because heaven, the home of God and of angel hosts, was thought actually to exist in the purer realm of sun and stars above and surrounding the earth, an eocentric conception. Jesus *descends* into hell because the inner earth is a place of darkness and burning on the analogy of the burning rubbish pits of Gehenna. By the same tokens the birth of a great man was expected to shake the heavens, which would herald his coming glory by signs and portents. The birth stories of Matthew and Luke precisely witness to the adoration of the universe before the princely cradle. And so one might go on.

146

Yet not everything submits so easily to this patronizing intellectual demythologizing. A brute reality intervenes. The crucifixion has to be accepted as real. But what a hideous death, naked before puritanical revellers, blistered by the Palestinian sun, defiled by the unconcealable motions of the body, doubly defiled because this is the death prescribed for a slave, and a death which for ever disqualifies a Jew for Messiahship or any other honour or dignity! Somewhere or other along that line the mythologizing process slipped up: where were the legions of angels who were present at the birth? Why did no one who attended that event cry out — or be made to cry out — against the murder of a divine King at Golgotha? Why did no one remember to provide Jesus with Elijah's chariot to sweep him from Roman hands gloriously into heaven? Why instead do we have the messy, inconclusive story of the empty tomb, and in several mutually exclusive versions? You see, there is a limit to the dismissals that can be made: the disentanglement of myth from record is probably beyond us unless a new biographical source is discovered. Yet myth-with-record also tells us much if we can shake our positivistic minds from equating myth with deception.

Of course, what much Christian exegetical treatment of Jesus has done has been to detach him from his Jewish background. All that which universalizes him, as the Johannine prologue does, plucks him from his locality. The answering device of some contemporary theologians is to divide Jesus into two: there is Jesus, who can be satisfactorily accounted for in purely human terms, and there is *the Christ* who exists from everlasting to everlasting, and Jesus is his temporal representative or paradigm. It will not do, of course. It is just a device to escape the embarrassment of the divinization of Jesus. But we only have the (*Christian*) concept of *the Christ* because of Jesus! No other reason for it exists! We cannot fish in the waters of Judaism and find it.

Then, the inevitable manner in which Jesus has been jewelled into the Christian reredos snatches the particular away from him. Demythologizing, by making Jesus a psychological symbol of universal significance to which we make a contemporary assent or denial, is dismissing the uncomfortable particular with such force as to say that the actual life

147

of Jesus is of no consequence. In which case the myth or legend could have been built around any crucified unfortunate.

The hardness of the particular! Upon reaching his maturity and embarking upon his mission Jesus makes for Capernaum! It is there and along the west Galilee shore that he gathers his disciples and everything begins. His one return to Nazareth is a failure. Why not Jerusalem? (I address the question to the first-century mythologizers!) He has almost certainly been there before, in adolescent piety, for *barmitzvah*. For the purely religious man Jerusalem would have been the right choice. It was here that the *beth ha-midrash*, the higher schools, were to be found. In the Temple courts he could have disputed the sacred texts with the learned doctors, breathed the daily sacrificial atmosphere, fulfilled a rabbinical destiny. Instead he mixes with the half-hellenized riff-raff of a trade route port and Roman garrison town, with fishermen, tax collectors, prostitutes, all politically disaffected, and probably careless of the minutiae of the law. All some embarrassment to the early Church. Political disaffection was no disqualification for Messiahship, but all other strands of that Capernaum life were. In politics, the acceptable Messiah could be extreme, but in religious and social practice he was expected to be as rigorous as any Essene. The ascetic holy man, John the Baptist, the uncontaminated, more easily filled the bill than Jesus who wined and dined with gluttons and consorted with prostitutes.

Again one has to say that Jerusalem rather than Capernaum would have been obligatory if Jesus sought to be near the sources of political and religious power and to test himself against them, surely possible before his own campaign had begun and the hostility of the authorities been aroused? It might even have been a sign of religious grace, like the boyish disputation in the Temple, to dissociate himself from the boorish Galileans, distrusted and despised in the capital city, and so acknowledge the supremacy of Jerusalem *like any other orthodox Jew*. There is a touch of obstinacy in taking the road to Capernaum, a deliberate decision to associate himself with the politically disaffected provinces, with Capernaum as a centre of vice and agitation. Baptism into John's movement must equally have been a political act;

Mark says 'all they of Jerusalem' came to hear John. Many if not most to be baptized. And baptism, though it was to repentance, bound people to John as with an oath of allegiance. Luke records that soldiers too were thronging round John before his arrest and asking what they must do. The mere asking was sedition. And John replied, 'Do violence to no man, neither exact anything wrongfully; and be content with your wages.' In other words, don't obey orders and don't loot, don't rape, advice which could be interpreted in only one way by everyone out of napkins.

The baptismal movement was a political movement crying out for the day of the Messiah and therefore potentially revolutionary. The historian Josephus confirms this when he asserts that John was arrested and put to death in the fortress Machaerus because Herod Antipas feared he would raise a rebellion among the people. The allegiance of Jesus to John was a political act of the same order as setting up a base in Capernaum. It is of course impossible to establish a true sequence for the Gospels. But if we accept that the feeding of the five thousand men gathering in the hills, the effort to declare Jesus 'King', the retreat to Hermon and the row about the Messiahship with Peter *follow* John's execution and are part of the confusion and danger it brought, then we are in the presence of a *political* Jesus. It is possible that this is the point in the mission of Jesus in which he turns from purely political solutions for Israel to moral and devotional ones, and what the Christian church has fastened on has been the spiritualization of his mission which followed, but even that decent rationalization can be doubted. Everyone was political in the first century in wanting to get rid of the Romans, except the actual quislings, the Sadducees. And even they wanted to save the Temple. If the Jews were to succeed, God had to be on their side: but he would not come to their aid without signs of repentance and religious purification on their part. The legions of angels would not be mobilized. So the *moral* campaign of Jesus could also have had, for most Jews, a clear political motive. Then, too, Jesus rode triumphally into Jerusalem where most people had to walk, seated on a white ass, to shouts of 'Hosanna to the Son of David' and the strewing of palms. He rebuked those who tried to calm down the royal welcome. So perhaps he expected the

149

heavens to open and proclaim him. What he got was execution by the Romans for the political claim, 'King of the Jews'. And if now the crowds execrated him it was perhaps because he had failed, and the anticipated messianic triumph, with God's intervention, had not occurred.

I am speculating (but the baffling Gospels invite it). What is beyond speculation are the glimpses of a necessarily political Jesus caught up in the messianic movement and quite other than the supposedly faceless Jesus who emerges from the demythologizing process or the over-sanctified portrait smoothed out for us by the ecclesiastical centuries. I struggled hard to make this clear in *Son of Man*; what agitated me most then was to establish Jesus as a *man*, totally involved in his Palestinian social setting, rather than a divine vision. It is to his humanity that I still cling.

We have not done with Jesus. If his political insights and allegiancies eventually faded for his disciples and supporters it must have been because they were dwarfed by his sheer religious genius. Indeed, the Gentile faithful of the first century probably understood less of the Jewish internecine political warfare of their time than we do today for after the destruction of Jerusalem in A.D. 70 and the annihilation of the state, political Judaism of the home country ceased to have any meaning. But God was still there and his word had more poignancy than ever, and what Jesus had to say about the quality of the inward life and the promises of the loving Father who held out hope of eternal life must have gathered awesome significance.

No one who reads without somnambulism the moral teaching of Jesus in those long early chapters of Matthew can fail to be astounded at their brilliance. Here is no rehashing of the Scriptures but an original mind at work, a poet and fabulist, creating immortal stories and epigrams all of which breathe the spirit of the hills and shores of Galilee. Everything appears sharp and newly minted and the appeal to the purity of a man's inwardness, over against a sterile observance of an external law, is reinforced by ironic social observation. Since everything in Judaism was governed by convention and new ideas were only introduced as commentaries on old texts, the informality, the audacity of Jesus must have rushed through Galilee and the Jordan valley like a fresh west wind after the sultry southern khamsin. He must have delighted his peasant hearers by his wit and humanity and country dialect as much as he shocked the orthodox. Indeed, if the moral teaching of Matthew and some of the mystical discourses of John are to be accepted as evidence of his beliefs, then we see that the religious giant was splitting the political carapace in which he had first covered himself and moving into a world where his fierce moral teaching could easily be felt as an affront to some of Israel's most sacrosanct politico-religious aims. It was one thing to emerge as the political spokesman of Galilean peasantry: that, if dangerous, had many precedents. It was quite another to come out of that festering Capernaum background and set oneself up as the moral judge of the whole nation and claiming a divine commission to do so. The effect of that must have been like the effect of Solzhenitsyn on the Russian Politburo. Who did this man think he was? This was never decided in his lifetime. It was left to the post-resurrection Christians to make up their minds.

4

'If Christ be not raised, your faith is vain,' St Paul said (1 Cor. 15. 17 A.V.) one of the earliest documents of the new faith. Resurrection was central to it, and not simply the resurrection of Jesus, of which the early Christians were certain, but of all believers. In the very first letter which Paul wrote, to the Thessalonians, he asserted the doctrine of immortality:

We believe that Jesus died and rose again; and so it will be for those who died as Christians; God will bring them to life with Jesus.
For this we tell you as the Lord's word: we who are left alive until the Lord comes shall not forestall those who have died; because at the word of command, at the sound of the archangel's voice and God's trumpet call, the Lord himself will descend from heaven; first the Christian dead will rise, then we who are left alive shall join them, caught up in clouds to meet the Lord in the air. Thus we shall always be with the Lord. (1 Thess. 4. 14-18)

151

Death was a greater enemy than the Romans, and Christ had overcome death in his own person, and by proxy for the faithful. He would return and reap that glorious harvest. Here was the messianic death wish on the world, with all its cruelty and horror, and the rising of the faithful above it into a divine realm where man was reprieved from the consequences of his mortality. In our day Teilhard re-proposes it.

The New Testament is about death and the longing to be spared death. The Old Testament, despite the many cries to God to be sparing, is never that. The Old Testament Jews walk proudly in the stench of those they have slaughtered, and, themselves defeated, lament that the Lord did not lend his right hand to their cause. The loss of a son, of Absalom, the death of a child, the fall of a hero in battle, and instantly the mourning cries, the protests to God, rise. But death as the supreme enemy, the final problem for man, is missing from Old Testament times as it is from our own. We do not greatly care for death and turn away from it with distaste. We bracket it off in our lives and contemplate the death of others even in millions with equanimity. As Paul might have said, we are dead to death. It is a question we might ask of the historic human consciousness, perhaps a Jungian question, as to why this cry against death, against extinction, rose with such force in the first century A.D. as to move the earth on its axis. It never occurred with the same intensity before, or since. There is the probability that we are as much inferior in the depth and range of our human sensitivities to those New Testament people as were the Old Testament Jews, though we are too vain, too complacent, to accept that.

We faced just now a political Jesus who became a religious genius. Yet there was the healer too and we forget him at our spiritual peril. Was he going to drive out the Romans? Was he summoning the nation to repentance and prayer that it might rise to a godly revival? The voice of the ordinary people, the poor people, so seldom heard, replied with extraordinary effect, 'Save us from dying.' The people crawled out of their fevered alleys, they were carried on stretchers, they touched his garments. Ignoring nationalism and religion (and exasperating Jesus because of this) they asked simply, 'Heal us.'

Jesus could have discovered his healing mission by accident. Healing was not reportedly a part of John's ministry. It was not to be expected that the fiery prophet out of the desert would heal. His powerful scorn for his generation would rule that out. Sickness anyway was God's punishment for sin. There was no commission to interfere. The prophets had sometimes healed, but rather as a sudden compassion or as proof of their powers than as a consistent mission.

Both Mark and Luke tell the story of the man with the 'unclean spirit' in the synagogue at Capernaum and register this as the beginning of the ministry of healing. The incident was quite unsought on both sides: indeed the man, mad or mentally ill and therefore unclean, should not have been in the synagogue at all. He interrupts, possibly with deleted obscenities, the public teaching of Jesus and cries out: 'What do you want with us, Jesus of Nazareth? Have you come to destroy us? I know who you are — the Holy One of God' (Luke 4. 34-5). Leaving aside the last sentence which could be redactive material, the hostility of the interruption is obvious. Jesus addresses, not the man, but the spirit possessing him, 'Be silent and come out of him.' And after a fainting fit the man recovers and is in his right mind. The story spreads like wildfire.

It is after this that all those suffering from diseases came to Jesus to be healed by the laying-on of hands. Soon his reputation was so great that crowds gathered everywhere, even breaking into houses where he was teaching or resting, until Jesus could no longer show himself in any town, but stayed outside in the open country. And there follows a record of healing and rescue so remarkable that it has been dubbed miraculous. The assaults upon death expecially get recorded, whether it is the living death of blindness, leprosy, paralysis and possession, which destroy a man physically or socially, or physical death itself. Jairus, president of a synagogue, has a daughter at death's door. Jesus visits the child and though people laugh at him goes in and raises her, healed, from her death bed. A dead youth, on his bier on his way to his grave, surrounded by a mourning crowd, comes towards Jesus. He takes pity, halts the funeral, commands the young man to rise up. He does so and begins to talk. Lazarus, dead three days and in his tomb wrapped in his grave cloths, is raised from the dead though 'he stinketh'. The resurrection miracles are the crest of the wave of healing mission. What must have composed the substance of the ills for which cures were sought — the backaches, the migraine, the asthma, the nervous breakdowns, the sores — in crowds so close that Jesus could hardly breathe, go unrecorded. They are too ordinary.

It is unprofitable to ask whether it is *all* true or untrue. The nature miracles demonstrate how any evidence, probable or improbable, was snatched at by his chroniclers to drive home the lesson of his divinity. One need not doubt the success of his healing mission, nor that it was unsought, nor that he was impatient with all those who looked for 'signs' in this kind of thing. Nor need we doubt that he felt that it got in the way of his 'true' mission. When he reaches Jerusalem and faces the challenge between his power and that of the establishment, it all drops out of sight.

No, we have to see this rather in the perspective of his century, which would have earned us the commendation of Bultmann. All those new Christians were certain Jesus had risen from the dead, at God's command, and walked among them and counselled them before leaving them to prepare for his second coming. This was the unassailable basis of their faith. For the oral and written records of the gospellers everything which foreshadowed this flamed into importance and the more the story or legend approximated to his own passion, the more crucial it was. So if a boy's corpse is raised from its bier and talks, or Lazarus rises from his tomb, the message to the world is clear: 'This he did in his own lifetime. Why should it not be done *for him* at his sacrificial death, by his Father, who had sent him? And why should he, risen, not do for all the faithful what he did for importuning strangers along the roads of Palestine?' It is what Paul reiterates — Christ is in us and we are in Christ and Christ has overcome death.

Thus the healing mission becomes important kerygmatic material for the early Church. *Was it also true?* The strange thing was that it never became an issue at his trial. These silences were so eloquent. It would have been important to show that Jesus made lying assertions of miraculous powers, that the claim to have raised Lazarus from the dead (which is in John only) was fraudulent. The authorities needed to discredit the standing of Jesus among the masses, and they were understandably irritated by some of the claims made about his powers. And John says that what happened to Lazarus was reported to them and the cause of another campaign against him. Breaking into a tomb and raising a defiling corpse to life smacked of occult powers, of a horrifying demonology. We can sympathize at the Sanhedrin's consternation and their examination of the blind man. Yet silence. The actual official case against Jesus, the claim to be able to destroy the Temple and raise it up again in three days, seems at this distance incredibly asinine. Any schoolboy could have told them that, being physically impossible, it was probably metaphor, hyperbole. Nor did Jesus claim miraculous powers at his trial. The crowds did not shout, 'Heal us!' It would have made a stir had he called Lazarus or the child from Nain to his defence. But the Gospels report that he made no defence at all and we do not know of any official verdict on his healing mission. Yet magical or miraculous stories must have aroused hostility and influenced public opinion! On trial, Jesus was invited to behave as a magician. Herod Antipas tempted him. He was blindfolded and taunted to say who had buffeted him. Crowds at the cross jeered, 'He saved others, now let him save himself.' So popular mockery of miraculous claims made for him helped to turn the tide against him, and the defence is missing. Simply lost?

What happened to the resurrected ones? One is meant to assume that they were restored to their full being, like the paralytics and the blind, and could return to normal life. No hint is given that they return as ghostly phenomena. Yet the resurrected Jesus is a ghostly being. He does not return to the day-to-day struggle and take up his campaign again. His presences are intermittent, unpredictable. He is greeted with wild surmise — is this really he? Isn't proof necessary? (One does not treat friends from whom one has so recently parted this way!) On the road to Emmaus he is even unrecognized. If it really is the Christ, it is in a transfigured body which Mary Magdalene is commanded not to touch. He 'appears' through closed doors. The sense that these are supernatural phenomena is present in the Gospel accounts. Mark, of course, the first recorder, says nothing of them.

Jesus treats his renewed presence as temporary and awesome, about which people have to be reassured, and uses a

155

time he knows to be brief to spell out the role of his successor, the Spirit, the Comforter. What the records are saying then is that Jesus died as a man on the cross and rose again as a God to ascend presently to the heaven to which he rightly belonged, returning to the Father. If it is of a spiritualized Christ one is treating, then the appearances could have occurred whether his earthly body lay in the tomb or not. It could be true, as Ronald Gregor Smith once wrote, that the bones of Jesus rest in the soil of Palestine. Death is overcome *not on this earth* but only in the heaven to which the faithful will ascend, as Paul spells it out, at an eschatological moment, the end of the world, the end of time. It is the putting off of the earthly body, the putting on of the spiritual. It is a very qualified — theologically qualified — resurrection of the body which is promised, far indeed from the simpler miracles performed by Jesus himself out in the open, on the hills and in the lanes of Galilee.

5

It seems a recipe for Christian atheism to subject the Gospel story to commonsense interrogation, for 'things fall apart, the centre will not hold.' What seems to be left is a manichean myth — the God-king comes in glory, he teaches, he heals, he reveals his divine powers, he is hurled down by his enemies into his grave and rises again above them by divine command, triumphant, unassailable — something haunting and compulsive, out of *The Golden Bough*. It is a story which universalizes itself, as all myths do, in the promise that all men may likewise triumph over their enemies if they repent and have faith in their God. Or in the even simpler universal truth that the higher the good, the more fiercely it is attacked by evil, and the less easily proved corollary that God makes sure that the evil is always defeated. Yet this is not all.

What would it mean if the Gospel story was pure invention? We do not face in it the simple, radiant, joyous revelation of God to man — would to heaven that we did! We have to face the most bitter humiliation, that the Son of God was nailed on a cross by the men he had come to meet and to save. Man

156

does God to death, the story says. *This is the meaning of human existence.*

Even if we were to call this a myth born out of the unconscious, and breathe again with relief that man had only imagined this deed, one would not be exonerated. The darkness is still intense. For that man should invent this, out of nowhere — or out of nowhere in his outer world — out of, only, his deep inner torment, would be itself a cry from man's soul almost too painful to bear, a cry telling of man's need to be redeemed from himself and to find God. It would be a self-condemnation. Man needs to find God. When he does so he kills him. It is true still even if we suppose God is only the name for the best in man himself, and we deny all transcendence.

If one doubts that the Gospel story is historically so (either that the Son of God was crucified or that a man calling himself the Son of God was crucified) one is not released. The alternative to these possibilities is not a bright, rational world freed from superstition and doubt, with the path of man made clear and shining. No, the alternative, if it is all lies, is the quite insoluble enigma of man, the thickening mystery of the protrusion of man's existence out of the void in which it was once hidden, the mystery of man surrounded still by the void, of his anguish that around him is nothing but the void, that he returns to the void. That is the alternative — not the abstractions of man presented by sociology or psychology, but despair that man's most profound emotions and hopes have no meaning.

But the Gospel story cannot be all myth. It is too knuckle-hard in its fallible human details for that. It is also impossible that it is all literally true. A myth has its corners rubbed smooth, so that the story shall not interfere with the message. The Gospel has not that polished coin glow. It is too angular; and has too many versions. It is much more like the work of men desperately trying to remember every precious word and detail, hoping that the more they pile up the more their convictions of that past will be confirmed. A mountain has fallen on them and they are digging in the rubble for the treasure buried there and weeping with joy and sorrow as they do for those who are safe.

There is never going to be any 'proof' of the Gospel.

Christians will have to live with that. Still the story changes if one works along a different perspective and believes that *God is* and asks in what ways he might speak to men.

6

The difficulty then, I suppose, is to *see* man, let alone to understand him: how can one stand back from being a man to ask what he is? As soon as one asks — what is man? — one is beset by theories about him. He is the child and image of God, he is the latest product of evolution, the odd consequence of biochemical change, he is the result of socio-historical forces, even of an amorphous and supreme History, and significant only in the mass. He is an Oedipus complex grown up and wary, he is an immortal soul, or a totemic creature, a reincarnated capsule of life who might yesterday have been a beetle, he is the net consequence of challenge-and-response, he is absurd. Indeed, he is absurd, and so are some of the theories about him.

Yet man came before all theories about him. He was there first. There was not first a theory and then a man to prove the theory right. There was simply man. Man alone, in all that immensity at which to stare, and of which he was conscious. One is tempted to say of which he alone was conscious, and this would be true in the grand sense, if we except God. Animals saw what they needed or feared: it can hardly be supposed that they saw a world, only their own setting. But man saw more than his habitat. He saw a universe immense and alien and started to explain it.

He needed to explain himself. By whom was an explanation demanded? By no one at all, unless we speak of human society, but human society is a temporal collection of *men*, so that does not help us. Certainly not by God, whatever God man has chosen. There was no point in explanations to God of the universe he had made, though there could be denunciations, rebellions. There were those, too, and moral demands and excuses, so the mere task of explaining himself to himself involved man in justifying himself to himself, which is absurd. And *to* the universe, for when man justifies himself he is justifying himself to other men and to whatever is beyond to which he believes himself, or finds himself, related. There always seems some beyond – the totem spirit, the Great Spirit, the Pantheon of Gods, Jehovah, the purity of artistic creation, the Holy Spirit, the discipline of scientific truth, history. And always this problem of explanation, justification, involves him in responsibilities. Rituals, libations, sacrifices, prayers, expiation, fasting, learning – all are other-directed. So too is the acceptance of a vocation: it is the acceptance in oneself of a call which comes from outside to the inside and of the discipline and sacrifice this involves. Man is caught in a nexus: he is a point of a unique perspective, as Bertrand Russell said, or one centre of a myriad centres according to Whitehead. And facing what he is inwardly, and what is inexplicable, he nevertheless explains. It is a task demanded as far as one can see of nothing else in the universe. Animals and plants have a self-sufficiency; even their consciousness is not an anxious consciousness: it does not ask questions about its presence or about the universe and it would not be ready to die for the answers, or for lack of them, as man is.

So man – or better, a man, any man – is unique, and this also flatters him, and uniquely evil, which does not. The existentialists of the Sartrian sort were so overwhelmed by this that they abhorred abstractions, even family, society, mankind, history, evolution. Man was simply himself. He did not ask to live. He was thrown into existence, out of nowhere, by no one, from which he would presently be as irrationally snatched. He was thrown not just into existence, but into freedom, and freedom without guides or moral rules written in the sky for all to read. It is only after he has discovered his existence that he can begin to search for his essence and ask what he is and where he comes from, and what is his destiny and what does he do with his infinity of choice, with all the possibilities of self-deception and bad faith his ambiguous situation presents.

I tried to look at man's uniqueness in *Persons and Perception*, beginning with a critical analysis of empirical views of man – metaphysical views, of course, in most cases – and going on to what one can understand of man by an analysis of his physical being. What comes over in an extraordinary way, if one takes account of the physicists' descriptions of matter, is that man, every man, is an explosion of energy into the world, and in ways genetically assured, a unique explosion. Since energy and matter seem finally to be interchangeable terms, an *incarnation* of energy into the world. Uniqueness means that this particular assembly has never been here before and will never come again. The sense of explosion — of being thrust into the world unasked — accords with what existentialism has to say about man, and what Jacques Monod has to say about chance. It would be quite proper to speak of a burst of spirit into the world if we ask what now happens to this unique creature — his struggle to socialize himself, to realize his humanity, to have joy and pain, to grow, to suffer, to die, to know God.

Death. One cannot escape asking again what this means. At the end of the Second World War a number of us came together to found the Personalist Movement in Britain. Jack Coates was the leader of this effort, but there were many others: Sir George Catlin, Sir Edward Hulton, Stefan Schimanski, who died on his way from Japan to report the Korean War for *Picture Post*, many humanists and some Anglican and Roman Catholic theologians. Our inspiration came from the French philosopher, Mounier, disciple of Charles Péguy, editor of *Esprit*, member of the resistance, unfortunately overshadowed by the genius of Sartre. On the humanist side, Lewis Mumford, on the Jewish side Martin Buber, and on the Christian side, Nicolas Berdyaev were compulsory reading.

Jack Coates adapted Personalism to his own eighteenth-century atheist view of man and Christian personalism shrivelled in Britain under his ferocious attacks. But for Mounier, a Catholic Personalism was a sort of Christian existentialism. With all that was said of man's freedom, of his obligation to choose in the absence of any certainty or of any help, of the necessity hourly to move into a future totally unknown, he went along. Kierkegaard was being read everywhere in Europe just then and the scorn that he had poured on the idea that man could be tidied up and popped into a box in a filing system and so 'finally' explained and understood moved us all. No social or philosophical system, or scientific analysis could wrap up man. We shared Kierkegaard's contempt for Hegelian system-making and the egotistic

160

notion that the whole universe was transparent to man, and that everything that could be known, soon would be, seemed to us ludicrous in its optimism. And the concept that changes in social systems could lead to the perfection of man, indeed all such Utopianism and social engineering, appeared to us the great twentieth-century illusion which had led at that point to human destruction rather than to any happy redemption. The atom bomb was the result of an unrestrained search for scientific truth; the massacre of the Jews in Germany's Europe, the slaughter of perhaps twenty-five million political dissidents in Russia in the interest of racist or class Utopias were the dark witnesses to the real human condition with which we had henceforth to live. Man was scarred for ever by this evil in the most optimistic century of all.

Mounier's Personalism was tragic, but not hopeless. The loneliness, the luckless freedom of man, was balanced for him by the dialogue he conducted with himself, with others, with God. The uniqueness of man was not the same thing as deafness or blindness. He was not something concluded, wrapped in a cocoon. The reality of the world was persons-in-relation. However much he might wish to hide himself away man could never do so completely short of self-destruction. Living, he was always in some dialogue with others. Active, he was linked by tenuous threads to mankind in the past and across space: and finally in every way to God with whom he was caught in the I-Thou situation of which Martin Buber wrote. But not in automatic dialogue. A true dialogue with another is a voluntary act; it is always open to reveal oneself or occlude oneself. It is open to God to reveal or not to reveal himself: to man to open or close his heart. Personalism placed a warmth and intimacy at the heart of the universe where Sartrian existentialism could only find emptiness and despair. How it captivated us in the post-war world!

All the same, as Mounier saw it, Christianity believes in the necessary tragedy of man's life on earth. The Passion is a symbol for man of the cruel and relentless nature of earthly life. Tragedy is man's shadow. The world is an Euripidean world and not a Platonic one. Thomas More's martyrdom was the point counterpoint of his Utopia. It is not simply that men's plans go astray, but that the very nature of a man's own life, whether successful or unsuccessful from a worldly

161

angle, is inherently tragic, 'for the good that I would I do not: but the evil which I would not, that I do' (Rom. 7.19 A.V.). It is extraordinary to think that this judgement came from Paul, the first man of the first century to sing and to live an overflowing, lyrical happiness in Christ! The Renaissance Shakespeare, who understood tragedy as no one since, said, 'The evil that men do lives after them, the good is oft interred with their bones.' In *Paradise Lost* there is the Satanic oath 'Evil be thou my Good'.

Man is born in another's pain as well as his own. He begins immediately a struggle against his hard material environment. Too early to understand, he is yet entangled inescapably in emotional relations with those of his own blood. He discovers his own powers in the measure that he finds powers as great opposing him. He discovers his own powers in the measure also that he is forbidden to use them. He learns to keep silent when everything cries out in him to speak. And, after all, his earthly life ends, despite suffering and effort, or because of them, in the annihilation of the unique and irreplaceable individual in death. Not death out of a clear sky always, but after the gradual intimations he receives of the fallibility and corruptibility of his body. Man sees death approaching far off, cutting off his escape. foreclosing on his achievements. 'Man has created death.'

Inherently tragic too is the realization which comes to man that in his greatest and most fulfilling experiences, in his supreme love for another human being, in the most creative acts of his hands and spirit, in the most humble search for truth or for understanding of the word of God, lies failure. The love dies, the creative act fails to answer the inspiration:

> Between the motion
> And the act
> Falls the shadow.

The search for truth ends in doubts, the struggle to seek union with God is haunted by incompleteness. All this dying is a preparation for the final moment of dying to the world. We die continually and, in the words of Péguy, '*quand un homme se meurt, il ne meurt pas seulement de la maladie qu'il a. Il meurt de toute sa vie.*' He dies of his whole life. Every man, said Rilke, carries his own death within him, as a mother carries her child, as a bud the supreme blossom which is itself a death.

Death is a process known only to living things. It is completely meaningless in any system of mechanics. To physics and chemistry the term is unknown. The most curious and inexplicable attribute of living things, that which gives meaning to the word *living*, is that they die. Living things possess, if we are to consider them for a moment as mechanisms, an advantage which other machines do not possess. They are self-renewing. The manufactured machine wears out. Its substance is in the end physically worn away: the parts fail to adhere. If it is too far gone, the machine is scrapped and that is the last of it. It has not died: it was always dead. The organism, however, sucks orderliness from its environment: it replaces the atoms which have become disordered by orderly groups extracted from its sustenance and so, minute by minute, renews itself as its parts wear out. More, it grows and reproduces itself. Its biochemical processes and those miraculous DNA controls about which we know so much, might very well, one could argue, guarantee to it individual immortality. Yet they do not. The replacement is never quite complete; the maintained whole, which is constantly being renewed, nevertheless deteriorates as a whole until in the end it loses altogether the power of renewal. It dies.

Death can put a period to life without this creeping destruction. Even a shock which involves no perceptible organic damage may impair the capacity of the system to hold itself together and the living thing dies. There may even be an actual decision to die, as in suicide, or a failure of the will to live. One has seen animals, as well as human beings, decide to die. It is of the most extraordinary human significance that Freud witnessed to the existence of a death impulse side by side with that Eros which one would have imagined to be the solitary source of human energy, for love and reproduction serve life and defy death and one might infer that this is the sole justification of living. Yet a death impulse, if it is more than senseless nihilism, argues that death is necessary and important, that living things need death, that life is only to be completed through death, that it is not a meaningless truncation, but a crowning of the edifice. The idea of death as unnecessary, as a hostile cutting-down of the living tree, as a process inimical to us which ultimately we shall conquer as we hope to conquer disease — that is death as disease, the theme of *Back to Methusaleh* — would then have to give place to the concept of life-death unity. 'Except a corn of wheat fall into the ground and die, it abideth alone: but if it die, it bringeth forth much fruit' (John 12.24 A.V.). In the ultimate sense, then, death is necessary to life. 'The wages of sin is death' might be construed biologically, 'the payment for life is death.'

Yet I confess that the balancing of life's books by the final 'payment' of death has a utilitarian ring which obscures the graver note of death. It offers an unreal consolation. That one lives and therefore one dies is rather like saying that if one goes up on a swing one must come down. Some events of life *do* have that kind of logic — if one is young, one can grow old: if one is old, then one has been young. It is quite significant that one cannot short-circuit growing-up, that, if young, one must face puberty, sexual life, love and labour before reaching old age, *but not before reaching death*. Hence the injustice of death, for which men condemn God, as when a little child dies of cancer, or perfectly healthy children are swept to death at Aberfan. Death does not belong to the *process*. To speak of it at all is to admit that one can come down without going up, that one can have one's cake without eating it.

Death breaks into the closed circle of life at any point it chooses. It lies alongside the whole of life, as the waters to the lake shore, as the invisible air fits the whole globe; it is life's other but unknown self and so something conceivably positive, perhaps creative. The new-born infant cannot pass instantly to manhood, but can instantly die. The existentialism of Heidegger and Sartre urges upon us that we are suspended over death, that our human freedom is freedom-towards-death.

Sartre also presses upon us that with man, *nothingness* gains an ontological significance. Well, to get away from philosophical language, nothing becomes real. It is he who says that certain ideas or concepts enter the universe with man. It was de Sade who said that in nature, of which man was part, there was only change or transformation and no morality entered into that, and so not even murder mattered:

death was a meaningless human invention! But Sartre pointed to loss, absence, bereavement, privation, mourning, all of which allege something missing, *not there*. Man alone perceives a something by its non-presence, perceives non-presence itself as a part of reality. Sartre saw nothing as a crack or fissure in being which profoundly altered the nature of everything, including man himself who ceased thereby to be a creature of the present moment or of the rough empirical reality immediately perceived, but a being always on the move, escaping nothing. For reality is pitted with the holes of that which is missing. But what is missing cannot be perceived. What other creature could construct its life round what is not there? Or build itself round some long-vanished event in history like the crucifixion of Jesus?

It is not only, if I may speak my own philosophy, that man's being is being-towards-death. It is a being-from-death-towards-death. The moment a man is born time is dying away behind him. He moves along on the crest of a time wave as perilously as a surf-rider. The moments earlier are irretrievable, the century past has interred itself, only an unknown future awaits him. Man is a creature of history too, but history is that which has become the past: he lives by this dead past, his culture comes down to him from it, he immerses himself in it, saturating himself, living by it until the dead past with all its conflicts, loyalties, hatreds is more important to him than the living present. The dead of the past manipulate him to his death in turn, as in Ulster today. Death there, in more macabre senses than one, is what the young live for.

Then, death has the majority, the dead moments infinitely exceed the present ones, the vanished suns the bright ones. The universe swarms with dead people, not just the famous or notorious ones of my halfpenny history book but all those unknown dead who bore their living suffering as patiently as sheep and who were swept away like the psalmist's grass.

I tried to express this sense of the omni-penetration of death in poetry:

165

How wrong to think the universe contains death!
It is the other way round — you must listen to me —
It is death which contains the universe.

Then:

How great the company of the dead,
How terrible the multitudes
Of the unseen empire!
How the tiered silent hosts range
From the lip of the amphitheatred stage
On which the lighted actors speak.
Do you imagine the living
Do not belong to the venturing dead
As apprentice to skilful master,
As infant to nursing mother?
Do homage then to Death's kingdom,
To the proud conqueror who spreads
Protectorate over the living man
Acknowledge the terrible armies,
The fluid battalions which traffic unseen
The brilliant thoughtless streets of life.

(Journey to Connemara and Other Poems)

7

It is consciousness of death in all these senses which sweeps
through the New Testament. If one reads it straight through
one is overwhelmed by the protest against it, the wave of
hope that it may be overcome at last. 'I am the resurrection
and I am life. If a man has faith in me, even though he die, he
shall come to life; and no one who is alive and has faith shall
ever die' (John 11.25-6). Even the order of priorities is
significant: 'I am the *resurrection* and I am life,' not, as
might be expected, the life and the resurrection.

Editorial? It could be — John's Gospel, so much later than
the synoptics, is passionately arguing a doctrine of Christ.
But if it is redactive material, that makes with more point
what the Christians believed was the burden of Christ's
mission and passion. 'The last enemy to be abolished is death'

166

(1 Cor. 15.26). 'But if thus we died with Christ, we believe we shall also come to life with him. We know that Christ, once raised from the dead, is never to die again: he is no longer under the dominion of death' (Rom. 6.8-9). There was, of course, a Pauline doctrine of death. Death came into the world through sin: it was the consequence of man's disobedience to God, the curse of Adam. Christ came into the world to redeem man from sin. Why should the redeemed *now* have to die? So, as Paul said, those who had died to sin in Christ, in Christ's death rose again to life, eternal life, in the risen Christ.

There is no gainsaying the blinding hope that 'death shall have no dominion.' But what did it all mean, since men continued to die, even the best men, saints and apostles and the childish innocents, and the apocalypse, at which the graves would open, did not come? Christianity slid away from the harsh and difficult bodily resurrection and came to accept the immortality of the soul from Platonism. The essential spirit of man would survive death and go to judgement before its maker: resurrection was tidied up and related to an individual's life instead of to the last trump. The doctrine of immortality in this sense, with all the apparatus of hell and torment, has exercised immense power over European history. When I was a boy there were two huge Adventist posters which stood in rank with Bovril, Gold Flake and Scott's Breakfast Oats on the hoardings: 'Thousands now living will never die', and 'Where will you spend Eternity?' They added a sombre note to my hurried, possibly breakfastless, rush to the station. We belonged to a European generation which still believed in immortality. The loss of that belief was like an amputation. We argued it endlessly and when, as a young man, I argued myself *out* of a belief in personal immortality I transferred my hopes to evolution with a euphoria worthy of Richard Jefferies. *That* was going on for ever, new species, new triumphs, earth and sun swinging endlessly through space in what I was sure was glory. I lost that hope, as I said, when I learnt that the earth was going to die and the sun was going to die, collapsing in on itself.

Years later, after the Second World War, I spoke to the Modern Churchman's Union on 'Natural Intimations of

Immortality' after they had cheekily asked me to address their conference 'on the physical, biological, psychological, anthropological etc. evidences for immortality'. As if *I* knew any.

What I tried to say was that with the old-fashioned notions of *substance* dead (in a philosophical sense), one could not easily accept the Cartesian notion of a mental substance which should survive a man's physical decay and so assure him a spiritual immortality. What had replaced it? I asked. I said that no one was quite sure, but if we look at Freudian theory, with its notion of an id which comes blindly bumping into the world, full of appetite but empty of experience, and of its transformation into Ego and Super-Ego, we can, so to speak, conceive of man as an inrush of energy or appetite into the world, as something quite new and individual in the sense I have already discussed. As though before his personal inrush *he* was not: so that he is something unique and not a continuing fragment of an old substance. Human activity is much more like a Bergsonian élan let loose in the world than it is like any *thing* — a stone or a chair — put there as it is and accepting passively the accidents of time and place, wear and tear. And there is just no 'reason' for 'my' particular here and now. Not only do 'I' come unasked into the world as 'my' particular existence, which I can never exchange for anyone else's, even the most loved one's, but I shall be deprived of it in exactly the same way. In other words, human nature seems also to be contingent through and through. But then the whole universe seems contingent through and through.

Contingent being is secondary being — it follows that it must be contingent upon other being, which is primary being. In the nineteenth century it was easy to say that the infinite indestructible universe was the primary being upon which human being was contingent. Who could accept such an absurdity today? Both man and the universe must be supposed to be equally contingent upon a being which is not themselves, but primary being. This makes it not only respectable but necessary to speak of God again.

If we add *time* to the mixture we see how contingency takes effect. There would be no contingency if everything existed from everlasting to everlasting. The fact of time is an expression of freedom also. The contingent being freely

168

enjoys its being in time. Freedom to enjoy means freedom to change. And time and change make death necessary. As Bergson said, everything is as if death was necessary for the greater intensity of living. A universe contingent through and through exists in time and in the face of death, and this is the measure of its dependence upon a transcendent creator.

But what of immortality? Here we observe the striking thing. Man is aware, as no other known part of the universe can be, no animal even, of his contingency. He knows that he faces the mystery of his own existence; he knows that he is not self-creating; he knows he cannot evade death. The mere knowledge of this state enables him in some degree to transcend it: as Traherne said, 'The contemplation of Eternity maketh the Soul immortal.' We witness in man a continuous struggle to overcome the limitations of time and space — learning, language, records, science, political systems, religions too, witness to this. Indeed in almost everything he does he seeks to overcome the limitations of space — from voices, signals, letters across space, radio, to communications satellites — or to survive the destructiveness of time. A civilization, a culture is an instrument to 'overcome death'. The voices of prophets and sages long dead come down to us as effectively as ever over the long vistas of time. Man therefore is not only contingent, but realizes non-contingency. He smells out the deathless, the immortal, and seeks to enter that dimension and to move in it here on earth. This is a theme I tried to explore in *Nature into History*. It really is a strange situation that man, through and through contingent, aspires continually to realize that which is not contingent in his own life and culture. It is an effort to fill his Sartrian emptiness, and is surely what Jean-Paul Sartre meant when he spoke of man as aspiring to be God.

I do not think we can regard this movement of man from mortality to immortality as meaningless, as a species of self-deception. It may very well be that man focuses in himself the movement of the whole creation towards the Godhead, and when I first wrote that, Teilhard's Omega point was still unknown to us. I am not one of those who think that the movement of creation in its element time is only a corruption of eternity and without meaning to God, who dwells in a still perfection. I believe that if creation moves in time, then time has real significance for the Creator, and if that which is beyond time has concern or care for that which is in time, then all that which moves in time finds fulfilment or finality in that which lies beyond time. The movement of time is launched at eternity. Man in his spiritual and intellectual intensity appears to stand supreme over all that exists in time and at the same time by his very nature to be called to that which is beyond time. One is entitled to infer that his earthly contingency is not the whole story and that his being is only fully meaningful if its trajectory moves beyond the dimension of the earthly and contingent into that of the eternal. Perhaps only if this is the case can man be considered a responsible being in relation to the transcendent God who bears him up. We can say he will carry the burden of his responsibility with him. He will enjoy an existence in and with the Eternal, but nothing in science or in nature can tell us what kind of an existence that will be. We are reasonable in expecting it, or in hoping for it, but nothing that is out of time (as immortality must be) can reveal its full nature in time.

Thus and thus I addressed the Modern Churchman's Union those years ago: it is on those lines that I would still interpret the doctrine of immortality as part of the cosmic drama of man's search for meaning and identity. The New Testament and the mission and passion of Jesus would seem to me to be the most powerful and tumultuous expression of a deep human intuition that if nothing lasted, if death was completely the end, the human condition was fraudulent, beyond bearing. And this was expressed not in the sublimities of natural theology but in the uncompromising life and painful death of one man whose history should have ended with the slaves's cross on which they nailed him. Schweitzer said that Jesus threw himself on the wheel of the world and was broken by it. True. But he also turned it.

It is of course, not only death in the final sense which concerned Jesus. There were the lesser deaths. The tapestry of his mission was rich beyond computation: the New Testament is almost like a series of shorthand notes, briefs, memoirs, letters, sermons in the decades following the death of Jesus, seeking to elucidate the meaning of special events and to assess the significance of a man whose impact was felt with even more force upon Israelite society after his death than before. It resembles in some ways the inquests which followed the deaths of Bonhoeffer, Schweitzer, Simone Weil in our day. Those saintly ones left a massive legacy of writings: Jesus left only his words printed in the minds of others; those closest were men of humble origin, self-taught, or untaught. The miracle is that so much survived and makes sense.

We can dissociate the unexpected campaign against death from the predictable campaign for the moral regeneration of Israel. The moral campaign is expressed with beautiful simplicity by Jesus himself in words, hackneyed in our time, revolutionary in his. It can be summarized in the demand for the interiorization of the law. There in a man's inwardness a man's own righteousness could be judged more effectively than by the law, and there the law itself was judged more stringently for its rectitude than by any other tribunal except God himself. What Jesus said about Corban showed that Jewish law had been systematically used as a cover for evil which left the culprit's conscience quite untouched. He could hold his head high for he was still within the law and the law was the covenant with God. Jesus taught a concept of good and evil which affronted Jews who could not think beyond the law: how vulnerable they were once the law itself came under moral judgement! Just to have accomplished that reformation would have ensured Jesus a place among the prophets, and a prophet's condemnation. I think it was Simone Weil who said that Jesus did not come to overcome evil but to enable men to distinguish good from evil, and make their choices. The establishment of a godly presence, a godly tribune, *within* every man, lifted first Christians, and then mankind, on to a new plane of moral consciousness. True, it is a tilting deck we walk now that the interior dialogue with God has given place to a hedonistic monologue in our secular societies, but the step back into a literal dependence on the law is now impossible for free men anywhere.

But if Jesus established a higher tribunal than the law, he contributed a positive ethic also offensive to a stiff-necked people. Love God. Love me and keep my commandments. Love your neighbour as yourself. Love your enemies. Be merciful: do unto others as you would be done by. Judge not lest you be judged. Judge yourself before you judge others. Turn the cheek, be a peacemaker. Go farther than the law or even commonsense would ask in the service of your neighbours. Seek to be servant not master. Serve God, not wealth or self-seeking. Lay not up treasure on earth: be not anxious about tomorrow. Don't worship material things. Cause no one to stumble. Live without show, worship without ostentation. Accept the truth when it is shown to you, no matter by whom: not to do so is the unforgivable sin. Be fierce in the defence of your integrity. Obedience to God comes before duty to men, if there is a conflict. Be prepared for any sacrifice, any suffering for the faith.

It constitutes a demand for a spiritual fanaticism, and made to a proud warlike people, boastful of their military triumphs, who were sure that the Lord God of Hosts, on their side in the past, would be with them on the messianic day of reckoning! It is rather like a corps of barefoot Franciscans confronting Janissaries and saying, 'Love your enemies.' The Jews smarted under an occupation which they felt could only be ended by military defeat of the Romans: so, what seems morally platitudinous to us (heaven help us), was socially revolutionary to the Jews, and probably unacceptable to some of the disciples, including Judas. Simon the Zealot, too, could have been a *terrorist* follower of Jesus, not committed to loving his Roman neighbours. So let's not simplify the complex, dangerous situation in which Jesus moved and preached, or his courage in maintaining his line, especially in Capernaum, that centre of disaffection, with an iron will.

Jesus was a poet. I do not find it easy to understand why

our age undervalues him in this role. Every poet and story-teller, like every philosopher, agitator, or traveller with wonders to tell would gravitate to the market place in those simpler days. Jesus was at the heart of this populist life, enchanting his audiences with those vivid, poetic stories based on their own lives and always with a political or religious sting in the tail. His mastery of popular language, his ability to argue the most complicated questions in stories and poetry which never distort the truth for the sake of the tale, reveal his genius. We should pay tribute, then, to a poetic fire and artistic integrity not often enough made. If Jesus was not Messiah, Son of God, prophet, or whatever, he was still a man of genius who hit his society like a bombshell.

One story of the husbandman gives us the lost populism. It is common to all the synoptic Gospels and is Jesus's answer to the challenge — who are you, and by whose authority do you act? Jesus answers by saying: address the question to John the Baptist before you come to me, and tells two parables, the second and most skilful of which must have seemed to his Jerusalem audience breath-taking in its effrontery:

> Listen to another parable. There was a landowner who planted a vineyard: he put a wall round it, hewed out a winepress, and built a watch-tower; then he let it out to wine-growers and went abroad. When the vintage season approached, he sent his servants to the tenants to collect the produce due to him. But they took his servants and thrashed one, murdered another and stoned a third. Again, he sent other servants, this time a larger number; and they did the same to them. At last he sent them his son. 'They will respect my son,' he said. But when they saw the son the tenants said to one another, 'This is the heir; come on, let us kill him, and get his inheritance. And they took him, flung him out of the vineyard, and murdered him. When the owner of the vineyard comes, how do you think he will deal with those tenants? (Matt. 21. 33-41)

If someone invented that about Jesus, then the mantle of Jesus's genius had fallen upon him. If this thrice-told story was his own then the messianic claim is unmistakable. The divinity of the mission is asserted, even the claim to the throne of Israel, in terms that imply at least symbolic sonship of God. It changes the historical perspective.

Paul makes no use of this fabulous material — he is his own religious genius who owes remarkably little to the Gospels which must have been orally abroad in embryo when he wrote. But it is useful to point out here how, under the moralizing Paul, physical death and resurrection of the body, the rising to immortal life, become an analogue for the death to sin and resurrection to spiritual life of the followers of Jesus in *this* world. Thus the resurrection of the body, the rising to immortal life, are seen as symbolic of a moral spiritual transformation *in this world* for those who have faith.

We know that Christ, once raised from the dead, is never to die again; he is no longer under the dominion of death. For in dying as he died, he died to sin, once for all, and in living as he lives, he lives to God. In the same way you must regard yourselves as dead to sin and alive to God, in union with Christ Jesus.

So sin must no longer reign in your mortal body, exacting obedience to the body's desires. You must no longer put its several parts at sin's disposal, as implements for doing wrong. No: put yourselves at the disposal of God, as dead men raised to life; yield your bodies to him as implements for doing right; for sin shall no longer be your master, because you are no longer under the law, but under the grace of God. (Rom. 6. 9-14)

As dead men raised to life. Death and resurrection become a giant metaphor for what might happen to a man in his mortal body! Such an ascent to saintliness must have made death an irrelevance because resurrection had already been anticipated! The martyrs felt that way. That is the astonishing paradox of the teaching of Jesus and Paul. A mission which preached release from the sufferings of this life and the overcoming of death by resurrection into a purer sphere also engendered a tremendous hope about redemption within this life through a new quality of being: a millenarian hope. It is as present in pentecostalism today as in the ecstatic early communities: the journey to the millennium began with Jesus. From a birth in *pessimisme tragique* Christianity launched itself into *optimisme actif*. I have often spoken of the difference between the classical virtues, prudence, fortitude, temperance, justice, and the Christian ones, faith, hope, love. The first underline the cautious and restraining maxims of folk understanding — look before you leap, a bird in the hand is worth two in the bush, a stitch in time saves nine, mistrust the Greeks when they come bearing gifts, and so on. Do not give in. Be hard to the world. Do not be undermined by softness, emotion. Keep your cool. Take everything with a pinch of salt. They promote the stoic disciplines of a soldier or paterfamilias rather than the heroic enterprises of Francis, or Columbus, or a Leonardo. They steel a man against the disappointments and outrages of the world. They hardly encourage him to expose himself to more. The Christian virtues, faith, hope, love, on the contrary, give hostages to fortune. How easily faith can be lost, hope confounded, love destroyed! In pressing these virtues on the Christian hosts Christianity was creating men of a millennial temper, full of the zeal of the Lord. For they are all virtues which throw out tendrils into the future. 'Cast thy bread upon the waters; for thou shalt find it after many days.' But as Ecclesiastes 11 also says: 'He that observeth the wind shall not sow; and he that regardeth the clouds shall not reap.' The writer of Ecclesiastes was in his gloomy mood, but for the Christians this was the stuff of their courage. Do not withhold your hand in the face of another's need or in adversity, or retreat from the opportunities the world offers. These became the mark of Christendom, by which the wheel of the world was turned.

PART SIX

The blackmail of perfection
GEORGE STEINER

1

Men were not, by and large, made new in Christ. The millennial expectation, the Kingdom 'on earth as in heaven', has
not been realized. Indeed the effort to bring it about has been
more destructive than the evils it was designed to cure. We
might bracket these failures with the fact that death was not
overcome. Jesus did not succeed (if he ever intended) in putting the order of nature into reverse. The old Adam is still
around. We might even say that if Jesus widened and deepened
the possibilities of good he created new categories of evil. In
these ways, rather than in the simple triumph of good, he
changed history.

For history was changed, and it was the effort to change it,
rather than any particular success, which brought a new
world into being. If no man ever became dead to sin, he was
often changed beyond recognition by seeking to become so.
New human types, the saint, the martyr, were born. The
fanatic too. Not exclusively Christian, of course, but very
typically so. One thinks of St Francis and Savonarola, Luther
and St Thomas More: of the Inquisition as the instrument of
a bureaucratic fanaticism. What came into existence was a
world, inconceivable without Christianity as its midwife, in
which man encountered his own nature with the newborn
confidence with which he faced the natural world. The Godhead was not hostile, intent on revenge: the universe was 'on
man's side' and God would intervene lovingly, justly, for
men, particularly good men. But his mercy and his grace could
flow to all men: 'the quality of mercy is not strained'. There
was a warmth at the heart of things and God was a caring,
providential God. Jesus was the emissary of God, certainly
in the sense that if you wanted to know what God wished
his relation to man to be then you studied, you followed
Christ. And Christ overflowed with love for man, he healed,
comforted, he counselled, he forgave, he suffered a defiling
death that mankind might be redeemed. Traherne has a phrase:
'God by loving begot His Son.' The mysterious Jesus was the
product of his love for the world. God was totally love:
'Being Love therefore itself, by loving He begot Love.' In that

total identification with man the nature of God was revealed. With that sort of God at one's back one could dare anything, be anything. It was in that sense that Jesus so widened human possibilities, so raised human status in man's own eyes that a new world was born. The corollary of immortality was inevitable. God could not let die what he so much loved and for which he sacrificed his Son.

There is an argument in Dorothea Krook's *Three Traditions of Moral Thought*[1] which I have always found impressive as a witness to the kind of change that Christianity brought about. It centres on the discussion in Plato's *Gorgias* about whether it is better to suffer evil than to perpetrate it. *Of course*, it is worse to suffer evil than to do it, the young men around Socrates say. Polus is brutally direct:

> If a man be caught criminally plotting to make himself a despot, and he is straightway put on the rack and castrated and have his eyes burnt out, and after suffering himself, and seeing inflicted on his wife and children, a number of grievous torments of every kind, he be finally crucified or burnt in a coat of pitch, will he be happier than if he escape and make himself despot, and pass his life as the ruler in his city, doing whatever he likes, and envied and congratulated by the citizens and the foreigners besides? Impossible, do you tell me, to refute that![2]

It is certainly hard. Socrates does not want to pursue the argument on the basis of who suffers the most pain, who is the happiest, but upon the basis of living with justice or injustice, and he pursues his case against a powerful opponent, Callicles. As Dorothea Krook points out, self-preservation, mere personal survival, is, in the view of Socrates, not the sole or even the chief end of a good man's life. Should all our care be directed to the prolonging of life? The noble and the good are not to be equated with saving and being saved:

> I tell you, Callicles, that to be boxed on the ears wrongfully is not the worst evil that can befall a man, nor to have my face and purse cut open: but that to smite and slay me

[1] C.U.P. 1959, pp. 25ff.
[2] Plato, *Gorgias*, tr. W.R.M. Lamb (Loeb Classical Library, Heinemann 1946), 473c.

and mine wrongfully is far more disgraceful and evil: aye, and to despoil and pillage, or in any way at all to wrong me and mine, is far more disgraceful and evil to the doer of the wrong than to me who am the sufferer.[3]

Socrates insists that the way in which a man best spends his appointed term is in the single-minded pursuit of good for its own sake and so that he may face his judges in good heart and with clear conscience in the hereafter. But Socrates can only *affirm*, Dorothea Krook argues, can only assert his doctrine against the contrary wisdom of the worldly.

He cannot prove it, he can only affirm it, and leave it presumably to the experience of mankind to confirm it.
   But this, which is enough for the humanist, is not enough, one feels, for the religious temper of a man like Socrates; and what Socrates lacks, one comes to see, is a revelation. Nor is the sense in which he lacks it (in the first instance, at any rate) a sense either psychological or emotional, that his heart aches for the knowledge of a revealed God and his bowels yearn for the voice from the burning bush. It is rather in a strictly *logical* sense that his doctrine requires and demands a revealed God and a revealed Gospel to complete it. . . . not to be reached historically until some four hundred years later.[4]

And she speaks of how the Platonic yearning, the Socratic search, for the mystical union with the Good becomes in Paul actual participation in the life of the Godhead revealed in the Incarnate Lord, the summation of Good.

For when the world with all its wisdom failed to know God in his wisdom, God resolved to save believers by the 'sheer folly' of the Christian message. Jews demand miracles and Greeks want wisdom, but our message is Christ the crucified — a stumbling-block to Jews, 'sheer folly' to the Gentiles, but for those who are called, whether Jews or Greeks, a Christ who is the power of God and the wisdom of God. (1.Cor. 1.21-5, tr. J. Moffat)

In defiance of Callicles it is Christ who counsels 'turn the

---
[3] Ibid., 508a.
[4] Krook, op. cit., pp. 58-9.

other cheek' in order that evil might not be multiplied and love given time to prevail. And it is Christ who against all worldly wisdom suffers the kind of death Polus talks about, and will not defend himself, nor save himself by breaking faith or any other exercise in self-preservation. He was followed by a long line who yearned for the martyr role in order that they, too, might witness to the truth. This was the glorious role. The judge and executioner, exhibiting their power and their pleasure rather than justice, were of the order Jesus came into the world to destroy. This was the difference between the Athenian humanists and the Corinthian Christians. It was a reversal of the natural order in this sense: it was now a declaration of war by the good on the bad. A refreshing change.

2

I find it impossible to dissociate Jesus from the consequences of Jesus. It would be tidy if one could look at all the evidence about Jesus and make a decision about him — whether he rose from the dead, whether he appeared to the living, whether he announced himself as divine or even Messiah, and so forth — and then to go on to consider the impact of those few short years of mission in such a small bigoted patch of ground, on the world. This is what, in a way, Schweitzer did in *The Quest for the Historical Jesus*. But even that mighty work of scholarship would have to be rewritten now, so much have the perspectives changed. Attending to Jesus now, one has to see him through the filter of the centuries — the liturgies, the buildings, the councils, the heresies, the religious wars, the painful symbolism of the cross. His shadow is a long one. Then, returning to the New Testament, Paul is already a post-resurrection Christian, a profound thinker, certain of his theology, proclaiming a cause, and the Gospels are the work of men as committed as Paul. They are not historians assembling the documents and sifting the evidence in order to 'decide'. They are preaching Jesus and that is the only task they recognize. They probably embarked on their writing only because the Second Coming was delayed. There is no way round the fact that the Gospels are the instrument of a new religious movement which is a mystery, which chills the heart with a touch of the occult, that dead men should walk.

I asked in *Son of Man* — suppose the resurrection stories were all invention? One then met another stumbling block, that a defeated rabble, bitter over the failure of their Messiah, fled back to the hills of Galilee and at some point gathered to concoct the resurrection stories and to preach these (and a lot else) with a burning zeal which led to martyrdom. And that no sick, disappointed, tortured man ever spilt the truth! More, that out of these fabrications a mighty religion sprang. It would never have been possible to maintain such weak, implausible lies with conviction. Not even rogues could have done it. These men were not rogues.

In the parable of the wicked husbandmen, which I have said is crucial to our understanding of Jesus's estimate of himself, Jesus asks: 'What do you think that this Lord would do to these men when he returned?' He expects the answers — they would be punished, disinherited, destroyed. And this is the true corollary of the great myth of deicide: that God would destroy the world which had killed the Son, or abandon it to its fate. This does not happen. Instead, in the New Testament, the cross is turned to glory, the death becomes the beginning of a new life, the evil of men the more proclaims the infinite love of God, that which might have been the terminus of God's interest becomes the beginning of a crusade for the redemption of mankind, a new startling attestation of God's love. What, as myth, the story could be saying is that God identifies himself with man even in the greatest depths of his suffering, evil and inhumanity, and that only in such identification is the truest love shown, and that only a beginning made at such a point offers any hope at all of atonement. One has to begin resurrection at the point where man annihilates God in himself.

A myth is a true story which never happened. What it exposes more powerfully than any other medium is the human condition. One thinks of Prometheus, Sisyphus, Narcissus. This too the Christian story as Christ-myth does, and as that is a cry to God. Professor R.B. Braithwaite, in his Eddington Memorial Lecture, *An Empiricist's View of the Nature of Religious Belief*, argued that the purpose of Christian assertions was to declare allegiance to a set of moral principles and to announce an agapeistic way of life, reinforced by stories calculated to encourage the Christian way of life. The empirical propositions in the stories could be accepted without belief in the literal truth of the stories themselves. Sensible, though somewhat timid or flaccid, it reduces Christianity to the status of a Victorian moral primer filled with edifying stories. Yet the Christ-myth has a total impact which is profoundly disturbing. It invites, down the centuries, a total rejection. It just is not *comfortable* in the Braithwaite sense.

It is equally troubling whether it is conceived as myth or truth. Leaving aside the problem of what a myth is doing wrapped up in material taught as literal truth when it was mere invention, (such confusion always blunts a myth's impact) there is the fact that told as myth it is a more poignant revelation of the human tragedy than of God's love, for it is a cry coming from man's side. But told as a true story it is a cry coming from God's side. It is about God's suffering and God's need of man in a world God created and does not control because he granted it freedom and in which he too must work through dialogue, discourse, example, persuasion, through the helplessness of love, denied always the human power of violence to impose solutions at the price of death.

Whether as Christ-myth or Gospel truth the stature of the Christian story is immense. It *is* revelation. If God has primacy for us, as he had for me as a boy and has now, then God justifies Jesus. And in his turn Jesus justifies God. Only a loving God could produce such a son. Could God be less moral, less loving than Jesus? Just so, in this tentative, testing way, cutting down to the spiritual bone, would God move in history (I have long thought) if he needed to, and so the balance swings from myth to truth.

I simply stand humbled. I cannot offer any solution to the traditional doubts about the Christian faith, I have lived with these as much as with Christianity most of my life. Nor can I feel comfortable in the face of an equally traditional Christian glibness or facility which wraps up everything so tidily. History is not tidy; the universe is not tidy either; it does not look as though God is inclined to tidiness. The universe is shot through with enigma, with darkness. Man himself, for all his *hubris*, is a mystery not to be bottomed, whether as to what he is in himself or why he is here. In that Christian world in which I grew up, in that Christendom from which I sprang, whose cultural creature I am, Jesus fills the sky. There he is, the man of sorrows, spreadeagled on his cross, despised and rejected by men, asking to be seen, and understood and loved. He is inescapable, irremovable. I have never been able to remain indifferent to that enormous symbol of human cruelty, of divine love, of God-man tension. The left side of my brain demands analyses, evidence, proofs, and admires in parts the scientific technological civilization, which is also my inheritance. But the right side of my brain, the intuitive side, focus maybe of poetry, longing, love and awe, commands me to kneel.

3

Yet faith for me has an intellectual, a metaphysical basis, which I have expounded elsewhere. The universe is a seemingly inexhaustible display of energy which proliferates into multitude of forms: this creative energy seems perfectly compatible with the idea of a creator — logically to call for one. As A.N. Whitehead said, there is the mystery of particularity — why it is this world, this universe and not another. Another is quite conceivable. The science-fiction writers manufacture new ones every other day. One has therefore to face the fact of creative decision. Then in this mysterious universe one confronts not only animal life, blazing with energy, fierce in resistance to encroachment on its integrity, but man, also animal, animal with a plus — self-consciousness, moral conscience, creative freedom, life-towards-death. The mixture is beyond description. But we can talk, and we do not have to be religious to do so, of the person as the highest known manifestation of life in the universe. Is that 'person' entirely alone in the universe, lifted above the mindless process which produced it? Or does 'person' represent something significant and inherent in the very nature of the universe and its processes, as Teilhard de Chardin contended? Logic again would demand somewhere in the process, or standing above it, that which is personal and supra-personal, even though he, God,

Creator, what you will, may not be discerned in the process apart from the fact of process itself. Into this situation A.N. Whitehead argued himself in *Process and Reality*, though he began from a negative empirical position. Samual Alexander's *Space, Time and Deity* was another work with a similar orientation. Even William Temple's Christian *Nature, Man and God* comes to Whiteheadian conclusions.

I speak of all this to show that there is nothing to prevent one from deciding that the nature of the universe posits a creator. The difficulty facing the natural theologian is to essay a proof. The universe does not look different or behave differently whether one asserts a creator or not. And the verification principle has these days bitten deep. So, a kind of metaphysical stalemate develops. On the other hand, if one eliminates a personal creator, a governing creative principle, one views the universe as rolling from one mindless emptiness to another, and both its true state, and man an epiphenomenon, a freak. In which case it would be better if *nothing* were conscious. If one adopts the logic of a creator then one still faces aesthetic and moral problems. Aesthetically, the universe is enormously wasteful, prodigal in its expenditure of time· and energy. If the creator were intent on producing beings with whom he could have discourse and who could enjoy him for ever, he went about it in a tortuous way. A swifter, more aesthetic process could have been found. The one we are taught to accept seems cruel to men's eyes. In fact man delivers moral as well as aesthetic judgements on the process which gave him birth — an extraordinary event, when only gratitude is necessary! It shows the paradox of the human situation that with man not only concepts of truth and error, but of good and evil, enter into (and confuse) process. Evil becomes an actual force in the human scene, a power to be recognized, a counter-force to the creator. It was the recognition of the reality of evil which drove the humanist and atheist C.E.M. Joad back to Christianity in the Second World War. And the presence of evil, palpable evil, often triumphant evil, has led many to say that this is irreconcilable with a beneficent creator or creation — though reconciled and dismissed within blind process.

If we think of the Godhead, as philosophy and theology would in the past often have us do, as an absolute — absolutely perfect, absolutely complete, omniscient, omnipotent, omnipresent God, static in his perfection, a divine impartial computer — then it is as difficult to deny predestination for the whole of his creation as it is to admit the presence of — the outrage of! — evil in its midst. Either there is a perfect God who fulfilled himself in a perfect creation, or (absurdly) there is a perfect God who was compelled to admit rebellion within his creation and strives still to crush it. For neither view has the saving Christ any reality. But if for a moment we forget the ultimate perfection of the Godhead and look at God in the biblical revelation we see the world drama of God and man and evil in a new light, and free from the accretions of Platonism. For the Scriptures, though they may speak of a perfect and almighty God, do not reveal him in stillness, but in movement, in a creation still unfinished. 'My Father worketh hitherto, and I work,' Jesus said. The whole creation 'groaneth and travaileth,' awaiting redemption, Paul wrote.

It is always God in activity we meet — in the work of creation, in the lifting up of the Jewish people, in advising, counselling, warning, punishing them, scourging them by the words of prophets or the woes of war and slavery, a God never ceasing in his vigil over man, a jealous God. We see God urgently bent to man, loving and chastising, but never sleeping. And this surely is what is meant by that title which occurs so often in the Scripture, the *living* God, God not simply as concept but as a power over men's lives. And this God never behaves as though everything were predestined, as though from eternity to eternity all was settled by his divine ordinance. When Christ, the long-promised saviour, comes the justification given is that God is consumed with grief for the fallen state of man, and knows not how to express more compellingly his anguish for the fate of mankind than to send his Son in sorrow and love to be a man that God's forgiveness might be announced to men.

How awkwardly the Jehovah of the Old and the Jesus of the New Testament fit into a natural theology! They are far too active, reformative, moralizing to be squared with a creation which when he had completed it, God looked upon and saw that it was good. But how well they fit into a human theology when immediately, with the banishment from the mythical garden, one has to speak of suffering, love, mystery, evil, death. These concepts, which enter into the universe with man, are meaningless elsewhere. Indeed who is there in the 'elsewhere' and how would he apply them, if we except God? And so Jesus, whether as Christ-myth or Gospel truth, humanizes the deity, brings God into the appalling human situation to suffer and to die because of it. The impact of that, once we are parted from our clichés, brings vertigo. 'It's God they ought to crucify instead of you and me!'

Does this reduce God's stature as one ruling in majesty beyond the stars? Of course it does, though we might also say it *concentrates* him. He becomes a beam focused upon that strand in creation nearest to him, made in his image, with whose destiny he has identified himself and for whom of inner necessity, he suffers.

. I wrote in *The Jealous God* of love as the bearing of the burden of another's existence and took as representative the love of mother or father for a child, and how, though shot with joy, such love was faced with so many inescapable burdens and cares. Too little love and the child was crippled, too much and it was stifled. There would be endless occasions when the father or mother, or both, stood helpless, suffering, unable to intervene, leaving the child to his or her own decisions and battles, because where love is over-protective the boy or girl ceases to grow.

And then I said that if we accept this humanizing of God, it was almost unbearable to take up this theme and speak of God *the Father*. For where one man suffers in his lifetime with a few who are intimate and dear to him, God must see all lives, and into all hearts, through all times, and suffer all that they suffer. And suffer, too, with that helplessness which the human father also suffers. And suffer sometimes as much in our acceptance of his love as in our rejection of it. (What prigs children can become when they presume on parental love!) For when he sees that we reject his love, he foresees what this may cost us in spiritual loss, in the abandonment of the humanity to which he calls us. But when on the contrary he sees that we accept it, and reach for it, he foresees what this will cost us, for he knows how we will fail and slide back, or convert God's love into self-love, and indeed how the more saintly the lucidity granted to us, the deeper will be our anguish at our own failures. He will see the good afflicted as Job was afflicted, as Simone Weil was afflicted. All this he must see or foresee, and never fail in love, nor ever love so possessively that he extinguishes the freedom he has granted us. That God must love, and nevertheless permit man to enjoy that absolute freedom which grants man the right to return hate for love, that must be the everlasting suffering of God.

Whatever the verdict on the historicity of Jesus, the Jesus story asserts that the living God cannot be other than the loving, suffering God, accessible to humanity, and, with terrible clarity, that if man rises up to God in his goodness, he can also confront and challenge him with his evil.

4

The most perceptive and admirable of prophets, George Steiner, who knows European culture like the back of his hand and makes our native philosophers and historians look provincial, sees the Christian story as almost pure disaster:

> Monotheism at Sinai, primitive Christianity, messianic socialism: these are the three supreme moments in which western culture is presented with what Ibsen termed 'the claims of the ideal'. These are the three stages, profoundly interrelated, in which Western consciousness is forced to experience the blackmail of transcendence. 'Surmount yourself. Surpass the opaque barriers of the mind to attain pure abstraction. Lose your life in order to gain it. Give up property, rank, wordly comfort. Love your neighbour as you do yourself − no, much more, for self-love is sin. Make any sacrifice, endure any insult, even self-denunciation, so that justice may prevail.' Unceasingly, the blackmail of perfection lies hammered at the confused, mundane, egotistical fabric of common instinctual behaviour.[5]

And he goes on to deliver a verdict which chimes with

[5] *In Bluebeard's Castle: Or Some Notes Towards a Re-definition of Culture* (Faber 1971), pp. 40-1.

what I said about the new categories of evil exposed by Jesus's demand for supreme goodness:

> Three times, Judaism produced a summons to perfection and sought to impose it on the current and currency of Western life. Deep loathings built up in the social sub-conscious, murderous resentments. The mechanism is simple but primordial. We hate most those who hold out to us a goal, an ideal, a visionary promise which, even though we have stretched our muscles to the utmost, we cannot reach, which slips, again and again, just out of the range of our racked fingers — yet, and this is crucial, which remains profoundly desirable, which we cannot reject because we fully acknowledge its supreme value.[6]

It is an impressive indictment. One sees, logically, that the millennial excitement of two thousand years is capable of producing a backlash, grim to a degree, which may already be upon us. But perhaps it proves too much? By sleight of hand Confucius, Buddha, Mahomet disappear from the world scene. The Hellenic dream of civilization, of a Greek millennium, drops from sight. Plato with his abstractions, Socrates with his negative *elenchi* vanish too. It is as though, to Steiner, Alexander never was and the Hellenic ideas had never infected Christendom. If the Greek dream was simply of reason and moderation, with no appeal to the impossible ideal, it is as bitterly disappointed as any Christian hope. Indeed, Christianity takes over Greek rationality: it is not easy to separate Christianity and Hellenism before St Thomas Aquinas: it is out of the question after. And Hellenism was not just a Platonic hope of the just and loving society or an Aristotelian project of reason, order and law, but the Euripidean sense of the human tragedy — fate or chance working inexorably to destroy the sweetest of human destinies; *hubris* bringing the proudest nations and individuals down to destruction. Ulysses the wanderer is as important a symbol as the homeless Wandering Jew: Socrates meets and dies by unreason as surely as Jesus did. Be temperate: you must not expect too much, the learned Greeks say. There is an ineducable, irreformable, tragic humanity to reason with.

[6] Ibid.

'Not to be born is the best for man.'

If we think of humanism coming from the Greeks as the inspirer of Roman awe in the presence of the law and of the modern humanists' belief in the dignity, freedom and reason of man, released from dependence on a supernatural being, then that too, as much as Christianity, has suffered shattering blows in this century, the century of terror and unreason: more even, than Christianity, which at least possesses a sense of human evil. Humanism had forgotten its existence.

It would be wrong, too, to assume that the mighty triad of Judaistic longing brought supreme evil into the world. Jenghis Khan erased cities and their inhabitants from the world without benefit of Judaism or Christianity. The Romans flattened Jerusalem and destroyed its inhabitants long before the conversion of Constantine. The Greeks had slaves. The Aztecs annually sacrificed the flower of their youth to sustain their gods. The Jews were experts in slaughter and called on their monotheistic Jehovah to join in: they fought in his name. Need I go on with the catalogue of known human evil? It is not only with Judaism or Christianity that the horror of evil enters the world or its antithesis, the longing for the redeemed man in, not just the good, but the sweet society. It is not even true that these have never been attained. They shine out in the histories of families and villages, of tribes and countries, in a Switzerland or a Finland, a Pacific island or a monastic community, a city-state, a Franciscan priory, a Taizé, a Schweitzer compound, a lay Little Gidding. In some sense this ideal community, this just and loving society, is always being realized in our midst, but it may not be seen, and it is not guaranteed perpetuity. It flourishes better in small societies and families and is difficult to translate into mass industrial ones. The good in man or society can soon be thwarted by the bad as Robert Owen discovered at New Harmony.

So, one has to approach George Steiner's imposing triad circumspectly: this could be another mighty historical abstraction in which to get snared. Yet I would agree that Christianity heightened men's aspirations and deepened their sense of guilt and sin, and bedevilled many of its own good intentions through its use and misuse of its subtle psychological instruments. Nevertheless the call to a higher level of personal and social life, to unselfish devotion to a cause greater than the individual without sacrifice of conscience was always there, a goad prodding men in societies caught up in the Christian fever of onward movement to God.

If the Christian drama of man, with God's grace in conflict with sin, has been abandoned in our time, it was often with the best intentions. The socialist ideal was to make men better now, in just and equal societies, without waiting for a problematic heaven: there was no evil in that expectation, but there was in the *hubris* of the attempts to execute it, to make men good by bureaucratic decree, by violence, by terror. The Wellsian dream of a scientific, technological man, dedicated to truth rather than to the squalid emotions of his mean little life — there was no evil intention in that, only in the nightmare of enormous powers concentrated in hands of the fallible few, unable after all to leave their lusts behind them. Yet in a way all such dreams were efforts to earth the demands of Ibsen's 'claims of the ideal', to secularize them and give them immediacy. In the doctrines of a 'realized' eschatology and of a world come-of-age and escaping the ecclesiastical nexus, a demystified world, certain Christian theologies have endorsed the ends of humanism and science.

So we have evil as intentionally sought and ideologically justified, and evil as the hapless consequence of a known and promoted good. We have time as bringing all down, death as a foreclosure, and man's life as a tragic absurdity, if one can bear the paradox. And we have therefore to revise the import of Steiner's triad. It was not only the millennial hope of a just society, a fairer life which swept these into existence, but the messianic expection of the conquest of time and death. The human condition was to be overcome. Jesus in his own life and death reveals how desperate that human condition is, and he is destroyed by it. Yet he looms over the world with the promise that even in his death he overcomes the world. The fateful messianic promise is kept in him. The audacity! The millions sweep behind him seeking forgiveness and the life eternal. Viewed in this light Steiner's disasters become much more than the product of Jewish neuroticism. These disasters (and the power to overcome them) are the product of the soul's awakening, of the longing which came with the end of primitive sleep and which the

192

Jew first articulates. 'My soul is thirsting for the Lord: when shall I see him face to face?'

5

What I have been trying to do in these meditations is to grapple with my own belief, and the person of Jesus in the light of it, and this has led me to wrestle with the whole Judaeo-Christian revelation. I see this as a vast historical momentum, inexplicable in some ways, and irreversible in most, which has changed the face of the world even for those parts of it which have never been Christian. I would accept that this has not got rid of the old Adam, of the primordial 'confused, mundane, egotistical fabric of common, instinctual behaviour'. But it has spoken to that Adam and made him aware or there could never be that 'blackmail of perfection' of which Steiner speaks. Christianity was perfectly articulate about this. Christ was the new Adam. The blood of the cross flowed into the tomb of Adam. Adam was deposed as father of the human race. The sinless one had taken over. By the same token the expulsion from Paradise was repealed: the gates were to be open to the followers of the Lord. Here indeed was the blackmail of perfection spelt out in mythology.

Perhaps it needed that blackmail to stretch man into a new understanding of his depths and possibilities. This is nothing strange to the existentialist for whom man is always an unfinished creature reaching to fulfil himself in a future yet to be realised. The consequences of the Judaeo-Christian 'stretching' were new doctrines of man and of God. God became first the One Universal God, then the Fatherly God, humanly incarnated. The first concept lifted God up, the second lifted man up. A new difficult doctrine of man was born. His capacity for goodness, love, truth and justice was acknowledged to be greater than he himself had guessed. His person, his individuality, not just tribe or nation, were treasured by God. His conscience, the word of God in his ear, was supreme. He could realize in part on earth God's heavenly community. For him death was not the end, but at death he faced his Judge to whom he would render account

193

for all his earthly deeds. Thus was founded the doctrine of responsible man, crowned by his conscience, set on earth to fulfil the work of the Lord, aware of the satanic temptations not to and to go his own way. Sinful therefore, yet redeemable: and under judgement, including his own.

In earlier writings, I have argued that man's understanding of himself determines his cultures, his societies. His doctrines of man do not spring ready-armed from the brow of Athene: they are the consequence of a dialogue with his known past and his anticipated future, with his society, his God, his understanding of himself. And what becomes generally accepted as the nature and destiny of man determines the laws, the *mores*, the educational systems, the cults and the culture. The doctrine moulds the society which moulds the man who in the dialectical process remoulds the doctrine and the society. But so deep, often, lie the doctrinal presuppositions that a society is often unconscious of the final sanctions for its being and its acts, and in sleep-walking changes them.

They are more not less important for that.

If it becomes the prevailing view that man is of little account, that he is a scrap of nature like other scraps, like a fly or an amoeba, to be used up in the evolutionary process and then thrown aside, he is likely to get the kind of society in which some men, Aryans, feel entitled, and are certain it is necessary, to treat other men, Jews, as of no more importance than flies or other vermin. This puts another gloss still on Steiner and causes us to ask what happens to the millennial dream when it suddenly appears or it is taken for granted that a universal process, evolution, is ruthlessly on its side? And what happens to man (and his society) if it is decided that he is the expendable unit of class and history, inexorably beyond all reconciliation, at war with all classes not his own? A decision that man is of such insignificance that he is a mere temporary manifestation of a vaster force, history or economics, a drip in a wave, can lead to practical demonstrations of the fact: an intellectual annihilation of man can lead to his spiritual and physical annihilation. What else has been happening in our times? But then the world appears deaf to this insight.

There is this to be said about the Steiner view — that when the high, exacting Christian doctrine of man is abandoned

194

the fall is like the crash of empires. What takes its place? Perhaps a nothingness, perhaps a corrupted, power-hungry Marxism, perhaps a pagan racialism, perhaps the doctrine and the practice of anarchy in which society, any society, is at once the victim, and the oppressor to be destroyed.

> Turning and turning in the widening gyre
> The falcon cannot hear the falconer;
> Things fall apart; the centre cannot hold;
> Mere anarchy is loosed upon the world,
> The blood dimmed tide is loosed, and everywhere
> The ceremony of innocence is drowned;
> The best lack all conviction, while the worst
> Are full of passionate intensity,
> . . .
>
> And what rough beast, its hour come round at last
> Slouches towards Bethlehem to be born?
>
> (W.B. Yeats)

It is not possible to fall out of Christendom into some kind of perfected paganism in which restraints on appetites have vanished but society retains its order and virtue. Pagan society had to achieve law: it did not hang from trees waiting to be plucked. One does not swan into a pagan orchard where the lyres are playing and the garlanded children are dancing, but into a condition where no one knows to what, beyond his own lusts or pleasures, he owes loyalty, and survival is to the brutal.

It was thought by intellectuals and reformers at the beginning of the century that, after a hundred years of industrial and social progress, the world was set for a liberal explosion into greatness. Poverty and illiteracy would go, tyrannies would be replaced by parliamentary democracies, the arts would be accessible to all, science and reason would be our masters. Christianity could help by committing hara-kiri. Not exactly the millennial sunburst of the overwrought puritan or anarchist, but a decent, British sort of step towards a more tolerable existence. H.G. Wells in *The Dream* and *A Modern Utopia*, and a dozen other books, was particularly the spokesman of idealistic young people who thought that there must be something more to life than serving behind a counter, as Wells himself had done, and were looking for the revolution of reason science might accomplish. And we in The Woodcraft Folk tried to live that dream.

We have had the marvellous, predicted scientific breakthrough — the conquest of the air and of space, of many diseases, even of birth — and an uncontestably significant spin-off in the rise in the standard of living in the most advanced countries. Things accomplished beyond the dream of the Utopians of 1900! But we have also had Belsen, Auschwitz, Babi Yar, Hiroshima, the Gulag Archipelago. The century that conquered the atom atomized the conquerors. My theme (my unregarded theme) in *The Annihilation of Man* and *The Age of Terror* was prophetic beyond even my own conception of its depth and cruel significance.

My much-loved Charles Péguy spoke once of *'capitalistes d'hommes'*. It illuminated for me in a flash that, in our century particularly, clever men had manipulated human masses as ruthlessly as capitalists their money and with consequences even more disastrous. Our century was not the first to do so, but it brought the art to perfection. It must surely have been better in human stature and dignity to be poor in Victorian England than young, gullible and well-fed in Hitler's Munich or Lenin's and Stalin's Moscow. It is an important thing to say that poverty (under capitalism, if you will, if that word is anything more than a sick epithet) is to be preferred to the capitulation of humanity under an ideological terror.

Yet neither Péguy with his *capitalistes d'hommes* nor I with *The Annihilation of Man* hit rock-bottom in the moral hideousness of the age. A new corps had come into existence, *les capitalistes de mort, les capitalistes des cadavres*: not the merchants of death in the familiar slogan against armament manufacturers, not even the ideological enemies of man who robbed him of his humanness, destroyed his spirit, but left him alive, but collective body-snatchers, mass grave-diggers for whom mankind had already become a random, nameless pile of bones and festering flesh to be bulldozed into a pit or incinerated in a crematorium. And of no more worth than manure. I am thinking of the Gestapo and the S.S. and the K.G.B. under its various protective aliases and of what their presence in our technologically brilliant century implies. Between them they have annihilated the equivalent of the population of a major power. While science was breaking and

196

arming the atom, they were indefatigably grinding up men. Anti-matter, the hole in space, had found its parallel in the human scene: humanity into anti-humanity.

Auschwitz processed three million people to death. Before millions one retreats, one cannot grasp them. Death becomes an abstraction. But there are two remarkable novels by a Jewish survivor of Auschwitz who writes under his death camp number, KA-TZETNIK 135633. They are *The House of Dolls*[7] and *Piepel*[8] and they tell the story of a brother and sister separately herded — eventually all the family is caught — into Auschwitz where each dies by a symbolic suicide, the boy at twelve, the girl at fourteen. As documents they are unique and irreplaceable. The fictionalization enables the lives of these two children to be traced through sexual prostitution and starvation to the inevitable organized death: not the decent homely death Rilke saw that every man carried with him, but extermination. What happened was that as the transports, mainly of Jews, arrived at Auschwitz they were divided into those for whom the Germans had no use and those capable of physically serving them. The latter were processed through the blocks of the camp, beaten and overworked and kept on such starvation diets that they would even riot to lick the rough wooden barrels in which the thin turnip soup was served or fall on any scrap of grass for extra sustenance, until they became *mussulmen*, a state in which only their bones held their dysenteric bodies together. In such a plight their humanity was gone. They were only numbers anyway. They were as unconscious as skeletons walking, unaware of place, time, heat or cold, even of the need to eat, and one morning would be paraded, stripped, and shuffled off to the non-stop crematorium, mere yellow dangling parodies of men. For those who had not reached this stage the daily terror was to see this state approaching in themselves and others: Ka-Tzetnik out of his personal suffering unbearably exposes this. The dehumanizing and extermination of these millions of innocent men, women and children was the *business* of thousands of other men and women who took pride in their speed and efficiency and expressed no

[7] Frederick Muller 1956.
[8] Anthony Blond 1961.

197

guilt. The units of the mounting curves of the production graphs were corpses. Had Germany won the war the boards of directors of *les capitalistes des cadavres* would have paraded in medals. After the daily massacre, as Ka-Tzetnik makes clear, they would go home to play with their darling children in the swimming pool, or listen to Bach, all cares forgotten after their good day's work. They were post-Christian Christians, too, who went to church on Sundays in their very best clothes, well-fed, but not yet driven as the camplings sometimes were to eat one another.[9] Auschwitz was the Inferno of Dante and of Hieronymus Bosch lodged in reality (it would be a joke to say 'come to life'). Let Alexander Solzhenitsyn, a survivor of terror too, speak for the Russian cadaver industry in *Cancer Ward, First Circle*, and the successive volumes of *The Gulag Archipelago*. Alfred Weber, that genius overshadowed by his brother Max, in *Abschied von der Bisherigen Geschichte*[10] spoke of something demonic which had seized Europe, destroying the labours and hopes of Christian and humanist centuries and producing the triumph of a sub-man, an *untermensch*.

Why do I write of all this? Because I burn with it, and will burn to my death. Christianity is not just validated for me by events of the first century, as I have said, but by the momentum of its historical onrush. If that involves complicity in the events of this century – anti-semitism, for instance, or totalitarianism – that has to be looked at sternly and judgement brought. An anti-Christian Christianity has been around for a long time. Better not to give allegiance to it if that is all we are getting. We have been warned.

Sauce for the goose is sauce for the gander. Future centuries, if we allow them to come into existence, may admire us for our space probes, but they will describe us as an age of terror and judge us by Auschwitz and the death camps of Siberia, and by Hiroshima. And by Ulster and Vietnam. These are the crimes we have to expiate before a future humanity and they are collective ones. They are infectious too. I confront, as we all do, an articulate younger generation

---

[9] Cf. Gitta Sereny, *Into that Darkness* (Deutsch 1974), a study of the 'innocent' Commandant of Treblinka.

[10] E.T. *Farewell to European History*. Kegan Paul, Trench, Trübner & Co. 1947.

moved by the injustices and oppressions of the world and which will commit any crime, even against the young and innocent, and any injustice to achieve justice. This is Weber's demonic world baying at us still. And this is the price we are paying for the abandonment of the doctrine of the upright man, committed to that love, mercy and compassion which Nietzsche despised, and under the eternal judgement of his conscience and of his God. One can only mourn that the blackmail of perfection was never stronger if we have to pay such a price now, and who knows what in the future, for living in a post post-Christian era.

Nicolas Berdyaev said it all with his customary intellectual vehemence:

> The bitter truth must be recognised that it is a natural thing for people to hate and kill one another, but a supranatural, and a spiritual thing for them to love one another and help one another. For this reason what should be affirmed is not natural right, natural ethics and natural reason, but spiritual right, spiritual ethics, and spiritual reason. The mistake has been made of relating the integrality and freedom of man to the primitive and natural, to sources in the phenomenal world, whereas it can only be related to spirit, to the noumenal world. Everything is determined by an act of spirit which rises above the natural cycle.[11]

6

It is not sufficient to rage against the world, which is much as Christians made it, anyway. It is necessary to make a case for what human society ought to be, and might be. As Péguy said, '*La revolution sociale sera morale ou elle ne sera pas.*' But the essence of that is — one has to stand up for the law in an age which undervalues it. There can be no good societies which are not also lawful societies, though to be lawful,

[11] N. Berdyaev, *The Divine and the Human* (Geoffrey Bles 1949), p.114.

like being patriotic, is not enough.

There can be no revolution which does not increase evil if it does not emerge as more moral than what it seeks to replace. The reverse has been true of most revolutions of our times. There is no hope for us in passing from one immoral regime to another. And 'more moral' means 'more lawful' — subject to the judgements, therefore, of universal values and in a Christian land to Christian moral precepts.

All the same, throughout the world 'law' is at a discount. We are familiar almost daily through the media with groups which break the law, sometimes with impunity, like the terrorists who held the O.P.E.C. headquarters to ransom in Vienna, or the Entebbe men. We see governments (U.S.S.R., U.S.A., South Africa) treating their own law with contempt and we are brainwashed by ideologies which assert that there can be no universal law, no universal truths, only the 'laws' and 'truths' convenient to ruling classes or power groups. If that is the case it is easy to go one step further and say that the law is only another form of oppression, its majesty a camouflage for injustice. The psychological ideologies which argue that it is impossible to speak of *guilt* but only of the confluence of the psychological history of an individual with special circumstances, or the philosophical ideologies which say that moral statements are only emotional noises of disapproval like a dog barking at the newspaper boy, all contribute to writing down the law. Christian theologians made their own devastating contribution in Joseph Fletcher's *Situation Ethics*.[12] The hub of that particular heresy was contained in John Robinson's remark in *Honest to God* that 'nothing of itself can always be labelled as wrong'. Basically, every situation behind every act is unique. Neither Fletcher nor Robinson carried the doctrine to the conclusion that, therefore, universal law was an impossibility. Nevertheless that was the *reductio ad absurdum* of their lawless argument. If situation ethics is as dead now as it ought to be I am sure it was the Watergate case which killed it. It was quite an existentialist dilemma to be faced with a man who said, in effect, 'My presidential situation exempts me from the law.'

I want to plead for the law and for Christian understanding

[12] S.C.M. 1966.

and backing for the law. Not necessarily for special laws designed to stop practices of which Christians disapprove or for the repeal or amendment of laws like the Abortion Act, but for the whole concept and meaning of law, which we (Christians included) so easily devalue. It is the Russian dissident or the South African black who understands best what it is to be supported by the law in a lawful society. He is without these blessings. We however can turn on the law as easily as water from a tap and we undervalue both privileges.

When Moses brought down the law from Sinai, he brought it down *from God*. Everyone understood what that meant. No one questioned the eternal significance of the law, the divine authority behind it. The law constituted the covenant with God and the Jews saw themselves in that sense as a people under the law for all eternity. They became law-making people, as Leviticus and Deuteronomy specially testify, and the lack of order and system in that mass of law is a tribute to the newness of the enterprise and to the Jewish eagerness to cover every contingency while the great creative enterprise was hot upon them. We have to remember how new it was.

We may look at this truly remarkable event socially too. What was happening? A people was being created; a nation was being born out of a rabble of slaves from Egypt racially akin but not even religiously united. And this task would have been impossible without the discovery of the law that bound them to God and through God to each other in a bond it was impious to conceive of breaking.

Why 'discovery'? Primitive people are bound by custom and tradition. It is a kind of non-oral law, often a 'felt' way of behaving, sometimes ritualized, rather than a series of articulated commands. It clearly serves primitive people very well so long as they are undisturbed, but if some calamity overcomes them the very tribal existence can be shattered by dispersal, or the death of a few elders. The exodus from Egypt was a social calamity in the sense of the destruction of the customary life of the slave minority, which had to work out afresh the terms of their common existence. The law was the product of this crisis.

The discovery of the law was a civilizing invention as important in the history of man as the written alphabet. It sanctified a new relationship between men, the common obedience to an accepted, consultable code. It faced men with an *objectified* law, standing outside and above them, free from whim and subjective perversions, because it was (potentially) the property of all, could be learnt by all, and spelt out their common nature and duties, religious and secular. It spelt out too the 'alikeness' of men and what were their several responsibilities and obligations. Those subject to the law *owned* the law; to know the law was in a way to own it: they were not simply units compelled to obey it. That common ownership, that redemption from fear, was the peculiar gift of the *objectified* law.

It is necessary to understand *objectification* as a historical process. We are peculiarly indebted to Wilhelm Dilthey for this, and have to blame Freud and Marx for obscuring this gift and filling history with demiurges and demonic forces such as a governing but concealed Oedipus complex or the responsibility of unknown or misunderstood productive mechanisms for the totality of a given culture. These are the real historical obscurantisms of our times. But the act of objectification is one of enlightenment: it frees an understanding or an idea or a record from the suffocation of subjectivism. The first such human objectifications must have come from speech. The moment a man uttered and was heard, *what* he reported no longer belonged to him alone but was shared property, and for all the time it could be remembered and passed on. And the significance of that hits us if we remember the awful impact of certain spoken propositions even today: 'The King is dead, long live the King,' 'Do you find the defendant guilty or not guilty?' — 'Guilty my Lord,' 'The Body of Christ keep you in eternal life.'

The objectified proposition is freed from the remembered or misremembered voice. Its tone becomes neutral. It can be read for what is said, not how, or where it is said. As written, it can be studied, examined, in peace and solitude, away from the tensions and confusions of personal encounters. Besides, as something which can be put aside with other records, even forgotten then come back to and consulted it achieves the status of an incorruptible oracle, a permanent institution in the human scene. Martin Buber spoke of a common 'something' which comes into existence through a dialogue between

202

two people. It is their mutual property, which either can explore or refer to, which would die if the dialogue dies, and yet is not precisely either or both of them. 'We have a lot in common,' friends often say, and they mean this field, and no doubt much more. If the friends embody this mutuality in letters and the letters are preserved and published, then the friendship itself achieves an objectivity. Others can enter into it in empathy, understand it and assess it. Or take a more striking example. The Second Law of Thermodynamics which speaks of energy running down except in closed systems into an even dispersal which immobilizes everything, and so prophesies the extinction of the world, and more, in some distant time – is *nothing* as an idea passing through someone's mind, but is a rigorous proposition, an equation, exposed to other critical minds, and so to falsification, when published. It becomes a corner stone in our common understanding of the physical processes of the universe. The civil law and natural law expose the same human impulse to objectify and so make permanent and common and out of reach of perversion certain human and social understandings and responsibilities. But once objectified in this manner, the civil law, like a scientific 'law', or any other common and open agreement, achieves independence. We do not have to ask about the frailties or even the genius of the inventor, whether he did not get on with his wife, or whether, as the playwright Osborne asked of Luther, he suffered from constipation, to decide whether his proposition is true. What the proposition says becomes part of that common cultural pool which creates a civilization or a nation. The supreme example of this is language itself. We learn it, but we did not create it. It belongs to us, but we belong to it too, for without it we are dumb. Who created it? We do not know even this. It is part of the very mystery of human culture itself that it should play such a divine role.

The Jews saw the objectified law as an enduring, God-given thing, the seal on the nation from generation to generation. We smile at the unalterable laws of the Medes and Persians, but the mere assertion of inviolability of the law shows how miraculous and sacred the coming of the law must have seemed to ancient peoples. The Torah bound the Jewish peoples in a law the breaking of which brought divine anger:

the common responsibility to maintain the covenant made them, in their turn, an unbreakable people. The next intellectual step was the discovery of the universality of law: that all men, irrespective of tribe, race, nation, class, had a common human nature which imposed on them common responsibilities and obligations. This was the notion of natural law, principally the contribution of the Romans, binding on all men irrespective of social or ethnic origins. It hardly operates now, even in the most civilized parts of the world. Yet that same law, which could unite you with the stranger, the outcast, the enemy, was, however bitterly resisted, an enormous spiritual advance. It said — and how alarming it must seem to some theologians — 'uniqueness' and 'situation' are not the only ethical answers to moral propositions.

Christianity itself was a source of, and support for, natural law, because it offered a redemption to all men, all caught in sin. It recognized all men as within equal distance of their creator. In a world ridden with the hierarchies so frequently described in the Gospels, it recognized none in its basic teaching: if it favoured any group, it was the poor and lowly and oppressed. We, Paul said

> have put on the new man, which is renewed in knowledge after the image of him that created him: Where there is neither Greek nor Jew, circumcision nor uncircumcision, Barbarian, Scythian, bond nor free; but Christ is all, and in all. (Col. 3. 10-11 A.V.)

And this creates immediately the concept of the universal man, immensely strengthened by the *imago dei*, the doctrine that all men are made in the image of God and are directly answerable to him. This cries out for a concept of natural law for it pre-supposes a God-created natural man, a universal man, beneath the trappings of culture, nationality, class and creed, who can only be served by a common justice. One should note too that many of the assumptions about man embodied today in Declarations of the Rights of Man and in international bodies created to interpret and defend them are natural law assumptions. Rights to freedom of conscience, of speech, of assembly, to national independence, to life, liberty and happiness spring from natural law conceptions of man which the legal philosophers, to our peril, have stopped defending. We are living on past moral capital here and even the professional protesters seem unaware of the ultimate moral grounds upon which they are basing their protests.

Historians can point to other developments which reinforced the Christian universalism and so the concept of natural law. The time of Christ (and earlier too) saw the increasing decline of the city-state, that warm, tribal cradle of civilization in which every man had a place and felt secure in his identity. The self-governing cities were swallowed up in an impersonal empire ruled from afar by godlike Caesars. What could happen to those cities was shudderingly brought home to the whole Middle East in A.D. 70 when Jerusalem was utterly destroyed and its people killed or scattered. Men were left alone with God. And this civic breakdown happened again centuries later when, incredibly, Rome herself fell and only the enduring city, St Augustine's city of God, remained. The law which men could not sustain, God upheld.

The situation ethics philosophers did not oppose justice to love. They saw as clearly as anyone that justice was distributive love. One could not have the nationals of two different countries rushing about and embracing each other like players on a football field to demonstrate their (possibly hypocritical) love. One needed treaties to define relations, ensure equity, and express amity. Besides love is a very partial thing, as perhaps the football field again demonstrates. To love one set of players seems to involve hating the others. Perhaps this is not love? But Joseph Fletcher (in *Situation Ethics*) uses just such examples of *agape* to prove his ethical argument. His altruistic (agapeic) ethic is, 'I will give, expecting nothing in return,' and his examples of this include the Kamikaze pilot plunging to death to blow up an American cruiser and its crew and a Vietcong irregular walking into an American officer's mess and pulling the pin of the grenade hidden under his coat. Since these acts of destruction against oneself and others are given as *examples of supreme love* one wonders how Fletcher's first law, 'Only one thing is intrinsically good, namely love: nothing else at all', can be sustained. His own examples tell us how difficult it is to know when you are dealing with love and not hate. Even Truman's Hiroshima

205

bomb is, for him, the result of an agapeic calculus on a vast scale. In a way then, for him, a sort of love excuses everything.

Fletcher, and others who followed him, though they did not oppose love to justice opposed love to law. It was, logically anyway, the law which was the mistake and love which had to replace it. Fletcher's sixth law (decisive to my argument) is 'Love's decisions are made situationally, not prescriptively.' But it is the business of law to prescribe and proscribe: if it cannot, out of love or for any other reason, do this, then there is no law. The Ten Commandments proscribe acts clearly injurious to society, to one's neighbours. *They simply forbid them.* You shall do no murder, you shall not steal, or commit adultery. They do so out of a clear painful knowledge of what men can be tempted to do and how offensive to God and how destructive of human society they can be.

Logically, situation ethics must take the opposite course and say that since every event is unique we can only judge it morally in the light of the unique situation in which it occurred. Sweeping prescriptive law will not do because it prejudges the act. And prejudgement is the really immoral act for situation ethics! 'For nothing of itself can always be labelled as wrong.' We can only judge motivation, incentive, after the act has been performed. (Go ahead and shoot the President. We'll tell you afterwards whether it was right or wrong.) But prescription after the event withdraws all protection from society, and it is the task of the law to provide just that. Without it society would disintegrate. This is why I say that situation ethics and associated wildcat Christian ethical philosophies were sheer disaster for western Christians coming as they did, in the sixties, when law and order were under attack from so many anarchic quarters.

7

The law, as an ideal concept, as the sign of the covenant between God and man, and man and man, gets reduced to actual, concrete laws administered by fallible men. So we get unjust laws, and just laws corrupted by unjust men, and laws observed in practice and defied in spirit and societies so caught up in a dry legalism that men are smothered by that as much as they might be by lawlessness itself. It has been observed that even the most lawful societies do not love lawyers overmuch.

Law sometimes seems to take the place of living and it was — is — part of the strength of situation ethics that it longed for an escape from the legal mentality to spheres of generosity and compassion, and argued that if these governed *all* our relations with wrongs and wrongdoers, all would be well again with man: situation ethics was rich with forgiveness and this attracted Christians.

And the situation ethics people would seem to have Jesus on their side when they attack a dry legalism. Jesus was as fierce as he could be about that. So we have to ask, on his authority, how the command to love ought to affect the law? It cannot mean dismissing the offence: that might turn out to be a way of loving the offence, or of loving the perpetrator, more than those who suffer from his acts. Indeed this is one of the moral disorders of our society at this time, that we 'love' the perpetrator and forget his victims. It is the 'fate' of the perpetrators which haunts our consciences: that of their victims blurs and slides out of focus. Perhaps because we can more easily conceive of ourselves as doing evil than as receiving it.

No, the law has to lay down codes of behaviour, and offences have to be properly established by due processes of law and decisions of guilt or innocence made. Only after that should the ethic of love operate as mercy, compassion, understanding. It is the special task of casuistry to establish mitigating or extenuating circumstances, to enter pleas for lenience, or acceptance of repentance.

But love *as* the law? The trouble is that love is so amorphous, so difficult to isolate. It is not easy to know when it is genuinely there and is not self-deception. Self-critical parents often do not know whether what they demand of their children, whom they know they genuinely love, is purely motivated by love or stems from pride, or hurt feelings, or 'what will the neighbours think?' We all have difficulties there, and if we do, how much more must we have difficulties with the Kamikaze pilots or the Vietcong irregular who blew himself and an officer's canteen to smithereens. Subsequent Kamikaze confessions seem to show that what they most feared was dishonour if they failed to volunteer or if their missions did not succeed. It does not seem easy to convert that fear into supreme love. The Provo terrorists in Ireland would certainly assert that their supreme motive is love of country: what they dish out is better described as demonic in its hatred. How difficult it is to assert that love is the motivator in these and other killings. We debase love and expose our own incurable shallowness when we do.

Jesus taught and sought love. Yes, and passionately, and this cut him off sharply from zealots and other killers. He clearly saw that love of country or of cause did not excuse every violence against an 'enemy' which is what Joseph Fletcher seems to justify. Jesus made great efforts to spell out love in non-injurious ways − one was to love one's neighbour as oneself; to turn the other cheek; to go further with one's neighbour than courtesy, or his request, demanded. One was even to love one's *enemy*. Love could be morally explosive but not physically explosive. He turned his back on the appeal to him to accept kingship. He preferred a sacrificial death to an heroic one as the more loving and momentous act. In every possible way, it seems to me, Jesus sought to break the love-hate vengeance cycle which governs so much of human affairs.

We should be quite wrong to assume that this meant contempt for the law. His own words contradict that. What he sought was to lift up the law morally: not to abandon it. Then he sought something which has proved immensely powerful and enduring in human societies − *the interiorization of the law*. Mere outward conformity to the law was useless if one was cynical or non-conforming at heart. Purity of motive was more important to one's moral stature than obedience on its own. Every man was to be his own interior judge. So he called for something extraordinarily difficult − the cleansing of the heart. And he calls for it still. But this means the purification of the law too, not its abandonment. This is what he meant by 'fulfilment'.

St Paul is our great difficulty. His sweeping attacks on the law have always been an authoritative source of support for those who urged a life of spontaneity over against the rule of law. And though Paul began by attacking Jewish ritual law in order to save the universality of Jesus's Gospel (there could be no salvation for all if every would-be Christian had to become a Jew before he could be accepted by the Church) he moved on to the profound sense that one effect of the law is to condemn. Perhaps before the law speaks of guilt, there is no guilt and a man is innocent. And once condemned, everything is changed, spontaneity checked before the awfulness of the law. The Eden-like sense of man's existence has gone for ever. There is a darkness in the law because of man's own darkness, which Jesus sought to illuminate through love.

Yet if there is darkness in the law, the darkness is always greater where there is no law. And there is light in the law too, and this St Paul must have meant when he said that authority is of God. For there is no political authority without law. Leaving aside specific laws and even certain countries, the general intention of law down the centuries has been to maximize good and minimize evil. What has clouded that aim has been the confusion of it with the holding of power and the enforcing of it.

Actions also speak. Everywhere, when under attack, St Paul conjured the authorities to behave lawfully, or sought their aid to keep the peace. When facing death in Palestine it was to Roman law that he appealed against the partiality, the venality, and even the lawlessness of local law. We are on very weak ground if we expect St Paul to help us to break down the law. We are no friends to Jesus if we appear to assume that all men are innocent or because of the uniqueness of every situation deserve acquittal. Jesus would never have begun a mission of repentance which ended in his crucifixion to a people as innocent as all that.

8

Where do I stand now long after that revelation in breakdown with which this book began, and as I move towards the night of my days? I do not burn now with the clarity of God's presence as then I did. One cannot stay on those heights, though Simone Weil strove to do so and perished on her Everest. There has to be a compromise between one's half-perceiving, world-dominated self and the dazzling transcendence which can break in so unexpectedly and by which one is judged. The homespun world wears a different vesture through such revelations. I became a different person.

In the days of my middle years, even in the dark wood of those years, I felt the necessity to justify everything. I had the philosopher's itch to reduce everything to an explanation with the feeling that the explanation would account for it. Well, it is an impulse which still works in me, and I would be perverse to deride it. But I treat it with more scepticism and look at myself with more irony, and more charity. I have one life, I tell myself, and it does not last long and when I have gone the unutterable mystery will remain. I shall not have solved it. Indeed, I shall have added to it by the mystery of my own being as suddenly forfeited as it was once thrust upon me, and without explanation.

It is the mystery of my self, and of the world, which more and more presses on me as I grow old. It is often a burden and a grief at a world which does not seem to learn or at a self who faces a past which is fixed for ever and cannot be erased. Yet it is a mystery which fills me with amazement and wonder. How can it possibly be as it *appears* to be I constantly ask myself? And half the time I can hardly believe that what is, *is*. Age has stretched my credulity about the noonday world to the breaking point.

Richard Jefferies stood astonished and grieved at the flow of people and traffic at the Mansion House. It was something beyond bearing. T. S. Eliot had the same experience on London Bridge where the crowds flowed 'under a brown fog'. 'I had not thought death had undone so many.' I had the same trial too when, as an office boy going home over London Bridge, colliding drays threw a badly injured dray-man at my feet. The home-thrusting crowds in that old brown fog just walked on over us, the injured man, the small, pale, samaritan office boy.

I have stood, Lowry-like, in London streets, and watched the hurrying and the idling people and the noisy children all with their schemes and longings, their joys and their sorrows, their unquenchable vitality, and thought, yes, though the clothes would have been different, this is how it would have been a century ago, and the century before that, each one of them living in an immortal moment, and as if for ever. And yet not one of those beings is alive now. All that intense consciousness has gone. And a century hence. . . .? Oh, it is a common enough practice, this contemplation of the brevity of human life on earth. The Psalms are full of it. But it is the mystery behind the rush of time, behind the seeming solid, yet ultimately fragile universe which stuns me more and more. The world is not to be comprehended. We are phantoms.

A speaker on the radio was saying as I wrote this that he felt that with more information about the brain, consciousness would be understood. But, I thought, we already have consciousness and do not need to understand it any more than we do the taste of peaches or (as G. E. Moore would have said) the experience of 'yellow'. The attempt to understand consciousness might be only to misunderstand it. Besides, who or what would understand consciousness? Why, consciousness of course! This is symbolic for me of the mystery of a universe riddled through and through with riddles, if the pun may be forgiven me. And if only for this reason, these glimpses through its strange mesh at the burning glory beyond are a consolation, a promise before which I stand in awe. The Old Testament Jews were right in saying that of God the word could not be spoken. But his impress could be felt in the flesh itself.

There was a day of dazzling sun in Los Angeles when I boarded a long delayed eastbound plane. I was destined for that hunter's lodge in Ohio, in which, before a fire which burnt half trees and under a roof from which snow thundered, and the ceramic tiles cracked like pistol shots in the frost, I began to write this book. The Pan Am plane was half empty and I relaxed in a solitary window seat with a wide view and watched the crumpled Sierra Nevada and then the snowy Rockies map themselves beneath me: these are visions of beauty which we owe to the aeroplane. We were flying high in perfectly clear, sunlit sky, but before us was a thin darkness. We were not waiting for night to come, we were flying at it and presently it began to look as solid as a wall into

211

which we would inevitably plunge. The shadows turned to grey, then to blue, then to indigo. I could feel almost palpably that dunce's cap of night the earth wears where it is turned from the sun. Presently we were hurled so deeply within it that the cities were lighting their galaxies on the floor deep beneath us. I was filled with exaltation at being caught up so intimately, so swiftly, with the spinning earth and its astonishing beauty. I was returned to those earlier experiences when, in a flash, by sleight-of-hand, the light of the noonday world became a divine vehicle.

There was another occasion when, far from well, but determined not to admit it, I went on holiday to Cornwall and walked one day to the charming church of St Just-in-Roseland, where among ferny grottoes an eccentric nineteenth-century rector has immortalized his doggerel by engraving it on the marble slabs strewn about the place. Luck for him, but not for the reader! One is assailed at every step by Christmas cracker couplets of impeccable morality. Tiring of this tombstone attack on my sensibilities, I took a footpath on the north side of the church which climbed and dipped round the side of the cove. The tide was out and the dinghies had keeled over in the shining mud. Two redshanks were crying in erratic and thrilling flight, though there seemed nothing, apart from my distant self, to disturb them. I sat on a grassy bank, quite alone, with no house or person in sight, and watched them through my field-glasses.

When I tired and relaxed and put down the glasses to enjoy the sun and the peace dripping as golden as honey over the spot, the transformation was as sudden and as absolute as it had been at Marlow. In as ordinary a place as the beetfield in which Péguy died, I was at the still centre of a turning world. Everything was shut out except the penetration by the eye, the light, of another world. What possible words are there? The words have all been said: they are worn out. At Marlow divinity shone through the landscape. I was not conscious of it in myself. At the altar at All Saints it seemed only within. Here, beside autumn-tired hedgerows and cow-patted couch grass, divinity was both felt within and seen without. It was not so much the presence of God or the entry of God into a spirit's emptiness and hunger which moved me as the lifting of all into an unusual silence. There were no hallucinating experiences. The landscape did not crawl. Grasses did not become forests of snakes, nor the apocalypse flame on Cornish shores. It was broad afternoon, not sunset. Nothing changed, but eerily nothing was the same. If it was the descent of God then the consequence was that everything was deified. In the end, perhaps, there are no words, not even stale words, for that which does not defy sensory experience but is felt at another level and transforms the being below it. It was productive not of happiness but of something more active and radiant in the spirit, a positive joy.

I was not a suppliant and not in prayer, yet swiftly the point where I sat became the quiet centre of a dome, an enclave, curtained from the world. There was an element in the silent moment which I now see was present in all such experiences I have described. I mean the lifting of care. Simone Weil speaks of the afflicted ones, those of us in whom a sense of destitution before God is strengthened, magnified by the wounds we bear for the whole world, in whom the sin of others is a curse in our hearts as great as our own sin or even greater. For our own sin we can do something, for that of others only bear the burden they did not bear. The afflicted — none greater than Simone herself — are a race apart, but every one suffers care. It begins with the baby not yet able to speak which must nevertheless care deeply whether the mother comes or stays, and suffers agonies of helplessness if she does not. It grows in the child who, unable yet to reason or to discover its real identity, blown this way and that by the pressures of others, must cope with the mysteries of its own being, the tensions and tempers of its relations with parents and teachers, friends and enemies — and goes on growing until in mature life we are more securely bound by care than an infant by swathing bands.

This ubiquitous care comes to be the only dimension we truly live in and it invades even our dreams, in grotesques of misery, humiliation and anxiety. Care is not suffering, or at least, not suffering out in the open which we can come to terms with, enobled even by that which gives us fear or pain. It is like the permanent pain under the temporary one, the untiring anxiety under the immediate worry. It shames us by the triviality of its manifestations into disavowing it — how absurd to worry whether the train will arrive in time, whether the letter was posted, or if it said what it should have said or what ought never to have been said at all. Everything is so ambivalent or rather so treacherous in the world: one can never be quite sure: too little effort and the examination is not passed, the book not written: too much and we are so stuffed with knowledge or information we cannot use it, or we break down. Too much humility or passivity and we become inert and ineffective: too much drive and we are aggressors, tyrannizing over others. Too much love and we stifle love itself, for 'each man kills the thing he loves' — too little and there is no living, we are dying alone, unable to make bridges to the separate continents of experience which are other beings. Care is the endless effort to stretch the resources of one's life to meet first this precarious situation and then the next. totally different, probably promoted by meeting the first care with parries and feints: always the effort and the shame, the recoil, the renewed hope, the renewed wariness, the evasions, always another stretch of the tightrope which is life to be walked, with spiritual muscles grown arthritic with wear: the perilous equilibrium is almost a definition of bad faith. But how can one, facing the death of a thousand cuts, the erosion of a thousand dark days of the soul, ever pause long enough to discover what an authentic life might be?

The undrugged moments when care lifts itself teach one what it might be simply to possess one's being in integrity, in some completeness, as an Eden-like gift, round and shining as Eve's apple. One then experiences the spiritual levitation which Richard Church described in *The Golden Sovereign*, and a renewed energy of soul which seems inextinguishable. It is to be born again into a new transparency to God and the world, for under the obsessions of care perception is itself smoked over. Pristine perception of the world is no longer possible. The bands and strings of care go endlessly about us: they muffle the sounds, dim the sight, bring down the heart with sclerosis. Our ever-anxious, ever-fretting, greedy egos pull over us a dust which blurs everything. Perhaps not only the gates of the world but God himself is only to be known in those moments when care is lifted and the windows are washed with a spiritual rain. In the moments of immediacy, enjoyed for themselves, not for what can be calculated or accomplished through them, we experience perhaps a pure release from temporality and so come to share in the being of eternity. This release is not to be borne many times, unless one is a saint, in a life in which care, after all, is only one burden among many to be supported. There it was though, care was lifted from me in a glowing landscape and I was, for a little while, one made whole again and reconciled.

Looking back, the moments of grief seem moments of prayer or of offering coming from deeper in the being than words can describe, and the moments of uninvited and incommunicable joy the divine answers to such profound spiritual hungers. However one speaks of it, here, at the least, is the grace of God and the fellowship of the Holy Spirit.